FIRST HOUSES

Native American Homes and Sacred Structures

Jean Guard Monroe and Ray A. Williamson

Illustrated by Susan Johnston Carlson

Houghton Mifflin Company
Boston 1993

To my parents, Dr. and Mrs. Keith Guard,
and my husband, Victor,
who have given me loving atmospheres
in which to grow in all our Houses.

—J.G.M.

To Carol, and to Ethan, Sarah, and Tanya—R.A.W.

Library of Congress Cataloging-in-Publication Data

Williamson, Ray A., 1938-
  First houses : Native American homes and sacred structures / by
Ray A. Williamson and Jean Guard Monroe ; illustrated by Susan
Carlson.
    p. cm.
  Summary: Presents a variety of North American Indian creation
myths and discusses how the "first houses" described in these myths
set the pattern used by the tribes for their own homes and ritual
structures.
  ISBN 0-395-51081-3
  1. Indians of North American—Dwellings—Juvenile literature.
2. Indians of North America—Rites and ceremonies—Juvenile
literature. 3. Sacred space—North America—Juvenile literature.
[1. Indians of North America—Dwellings. 2. Indians of North
America—Rites and ceremonies. 3. Indians of North America—
Legends. 4. Creation—Folklore. 5. Sacred space—North America.]
I. Monroe, Jean Guard. II. Carlson, Susan, ill. III. Title.
E78.D9W55 1993   92-34900
299'.72—dc20   CIP
              AC

Printed in the United States of America

VB 10 9 8 7 6 5 4 3 2 1

Contents

Acknowledgments   v

Preface   vii

1   The People of the Longhouse: The Iroquois League   1

2   A Gift of the Gods: The Navajo Hogan   17

3   Emergence from the Underworld: The Pueblo Kiva   27

4   Shade and Shelter: Mohave Houses   39

5   Sun's Crystal House: California House Myths   47

6   Painted Planks and Totem Poles: Northwest Coast Dwellings   69

7   Painted Tipis: House Legends of the Plains   90

8   Models of the World: Pawnee Earth Lodges   106

9   The Big House: A Delaware Ceremonial Dwelling   118

10   The First Sweatlodge   123

Glossary   139

Suggested Further Reading   144

Bibliography   145

Index   148

Acknowledgments

Many individuals assisted us in making this book possible. First and foremost, we thank the tribal members who have shared these stories over the years. Their creativity and vision have produced stories of timeless interest. We thank Carol Carnett, who took time from a busy schedule to review the manuscript while it was in progress. Mary Kay Davies and the other staff of the Smithsonian Anthropological Library were extremely helpful in tracking down obscure references. The staff of the Annapolis Branch of the Anne Arundel County Library system worked wonders in obtaining books through the interlibrary loan system.

We thank Matilda Welter, our editor at Houghton Mifflin, for her many constructive editorial suggestions and guidance, and especially for her patience. We deeply appreciate the efforts of the copy editor, book designer, and other members of the Houghton Mifflin staff who have made this book possible.

Finally, our respective spouses, Victor Berroterán and Carol Carnett, deserve special thanks and appreciation for putting up with the many hours we spent in the library or at the word processor completing this book. Their loving support was essential.

Preface

Who built the first house? Native American creation myths reveal fascinating stories about the "first" houses, which the tribes use as patterns for their homes and ritual structures. From the Iroquois Longhouse to the Navajo Hogan, the Bella Coola House of Myths to the Mohave Ramada, Native Americans construct their traditional dwellings and sacred buildings according to cosmic patterns given by the gods.

Myths of the First House are a common part of most Native American traditions. They are set in the Beginning Time when the earth was young. In those days animals talked and shared other human characteristics; they helped to shape the world, create the calendar, provide foods, and build the First Houses.

Warm in the winter and cool in the summer, Native American houses reflect the skills and cultures of their builders. The responses of groups throughout North America to the challenge of providing adequate shelter differed greatly. In the Southwest, where wood was scarce, the Pueblo Indians built with stone and adobe, and the Navajo used logs and mud. Along the heavily forested Northwest Coast, cedar was preferred. Tradition also played an important part in the form houses took — tribal groups in the same environment often chose quite different ways to express their need for shelter.

Native Americans who live by their traditional beliefs hold that humans are an integral part of nature and should strive for harmony with it. Most Native American houses and sacred structures were built to reflect the patterns of the

1 The People of the Longhouse
The Iroquois League

The Iroquois heartland, south of Lake Ontario in what is now New York State, contains some of the richest farmland and forests in North America. The five Iroquois tribes — the Cayuga, the Mohawk, the Seneca, the Oneida, and the Onondaga — once prospered in this bountiful land. They also prospered politically. The longhouse was the Iroquois' principal dwelling before Europeans arrived in North America, and it made a powerful image for their political union. As the Iroquois saw it, the longhouse that unified their tribes stretched east to the lands of the Mohawk and west to Seneca territory.

The Iroquois people enjoyed a varied and beautiful landscape of lakes and streams, forests and meadows, mountains and valleys. They made good use of their abundant resources. Before the new customs brought by European settlers began to change the Iroquois way of life, the women planted and tended the crops in village fields, growing corn, beans, and squash. The Iroquois called these crops the three sisters because they were mainstays of the people's diet. The men fished in the lakes and streams and hunted in the forests. The thick, dark woods provided a wide variety of game animals, plants, fruits, and nuts. They also supplied the setting for a rich mythology and folklore, based on a belief in the "Little People" and various animal and other spirits who lived and played in the forest.

As with most Native American peoples, nearly everything in the Iroquois landscape had a sacred meaning. The elm trees that grew so thick in the forests provided wood for the longhouses and bark for house shingles, canoes, and baskets. Elms were also revered as a symbol of the unity of the world. Rooted at the center of the earth, its branches soaring to the sky, the elm assured a connection between humans on earth and the sky beings above. It was a cosmic tree that had roots in each of the four directions — east, south, west, and north.

Corn provided the Iroquois with a source of nutrition that could be stored readily and used during the winter months. Corn is so important that it is still the center of a key religious ceremony. This Green Corn Festival, which usually takes place in early August, celebrates the first ripe corn and gives the Iroquois the opportunity to honor the Corn Mother, who, as they believe, brought this food to the people.

Although Iroquois society as a whole is vastly different today from what it was even a hundred years ago, some of these sacred notions still apply, especially among those who follow traditional ways. Much was lost when Iroquois society began to change in the eighteenth century, because the changes were massive and swift. By the end of the nineteenth century, the traditional longhouse had nearly disappeared as a family dwelling. Fortunately, a few early European explorers described them when they wrote about their experiences in Iroquois country.

What the early settlers saw when they first came upon an Iroquois settlement was a large clearing on high ground in the middle of a thick forest. At the center of the clearing was a village surrounded by planted fields and a strong wooden stockade, perhaps twenty or more feet high. A village might have ten to twenty houses, each of which might be fifty to a hundred fifty feet long. These "longhouses," as the explorers called them, were often fifteen to twenty feet tall and some twenty feet wide.

In building a longhouse, the Iroquois started with a rectangular frame of poles set in the ground and tied them together with strips of the inner bark of the slippery elm. They framed the roof with poles that stretched in an arc from one side of the house to the other. Iroquois builders sheathed their longhouses with long slabs of dried elm bark, peeled from the trees in the late spring when the sap was rising. The slabs of bark were punctured with a bone awl and tied to the framework with flexible strips of slippery elm. Each successive slab overlapped the one below it to shed both rain and snow.

As the early visitors to the Iroquois wrote, these carefully constructed dwellings housed several families. They had a door at each end, but no openings along the sides. Above each door was a carving of the house's ancestral animal, or totem. A central corridor extended from the front to the back door, and families lived along the sides in rooms opening off this passageway. Cooking fires every twenty feet or so along the corridor served two families, who lived across from each other. The families' personal space consisted of tiers of low sleeping platforms tied to upright posts that extended from the floor to the ceiling. The families kept personal items in the space below. Above the platforms, shelves tied to the same upright posts might hold baskets, mats, dried food, tobacco, or weapons.

Because these dwellings had no windows, the only source of light in the smoky interior was from the smoke holes in the roof and from the cooking fires that always burned in one or another hearth of the structure. The longhouse families took turns keeping a pot of corn or meat stew going throughout the day to feed the residents. The side posts and roof beams supported strings of drying fish and corn.

The Origin of the False Face Society

Although Iroquois tribes no longer live in the longhouse, it is still important to their community life. Today's longhouse looks rather different from the one that was in use when the first European explorers hiked through Iroquois territory, but it still serves important functions. Community houses, today's longhouses, are used for religious ceremonies and community meetings. Both uses of the longhouse help support Iroquois tradition.

The False Faces and Husk Faces, as well as the healing ceremonies they take part in, are an important part of Iroquois tradition, closely connected with the longhouse. False Faces, made from wood, and Husk Faces, made from cornhusks,

represent healing spirits. The Iroquois believe that when male members of the medicine society put on these sacred masks they take on the power of the masks and are able to cure illness. Traditional Iroquois believe that illness comes about when evil supernatural beings bring disorder to the world. The False Faces are able to help heal the disorder that settles in a human being, causing illness.

Every spring and fall, in a ceremony called the Traveling Rite, the False Faces visit the homes of those who follow Iroquois religious tradition and ceremonially sweep diseases from their houses. In thanks, they are given gifts of Indian tobacco, which the False Faces value highly. Then they and the people go to the longhouse for more religious ceremonies and a feast. At the feast, cornmeal mush, corn soup, and cornmeal cakes with huckleberries are served, foods that are highly valued by the False Faces and Husk Faces.

The following myth of the origin of the False Face Society
relates one version of how the False Face, Old Broken Nose,
came into being.

When the world was new, after the creation of most things, Hawennihyoh took
a walk to admire all that he had made. His creations were beautiful, and he was
proud of himself. All of a sudden, Hawennihyoh came face to face with another
being. He was startled! As far as he knew, he was the only one on earth.

The other being looked nearly as surprised as Hawennihyoh. He stared with
his mouth open. "Who are you? Where do you come from?"

Gathering his wits, Hawennihyoh looked directly at the intruder and said, "I
am Hawennihyoh and I am inspecting all that is growing here on earth. And
who are you?"

"I am Sagodyowehgowah." Hawennihyoh remained silent. The intruder
slowly drew himself to his full height, straightened his clothes, and continued.
"I am the wind spirit. I move all things and I travel about from sunset to sunrise. I am most powerful."

When Hawennihyoh still kept silent, Sagodyowehgowah again asked him,
"What are you doing here on earth?"

"I am the one who made all things — the crawling, walking, flying, and
swimming things. I have made them all. I perceive that you challenge my
power." Hawennihyoh paused. "Let us have a contest to determine who is most
powerful."

Sagodyowehgowah agreed. He shook a huge turtle rattle and made a great
noise, hoping to frighten and intimidate Hawennihyoh.

"I am not afraid of your noise," said Hawennihyoh. "Let the contest begin.
Let us face away from this mountain. Whichever of us that can make the
mountain move, he is the one with the most power. Neither of us must turn
around to look at the mountain before the contest is over."

Sagodyowehgowah agreed. Then they both turned their backs to the mountain.

Sagodyowehgowah went first. "Mountain, I command you to walk toward us!"

The mountain trembled and groaned but moved only a little. Then the mountain stopped and refused to move farther.

Now it was Hawennihyoh's turn to demonstrate his power. He also commanded the mountain to walk toward them.

Just then Sagodyowehgowah heard a strange noise and, although he had agreed not to turn around during the contest, the sound startled him. He twisted his head suddenly. As he turned, his face scraped against the mountain cliff that had stopped just behind him. "Ow!" he shouted. "That hurt!" The force was great enough to shift his entire face. Twisted and distorted, Sagodyowehgowah turned back and looked into the eyes of his antagonist.

Hawennihyoh said, "You see, I created everything here. I am master of these things. Even the mountain obeys me."

Seeing the twisted face of Sagodyowehgowah, Hawennihyoh asked, "What happened to you? Why are you so twisted?"

Sagodyowehgowah's face looked even more twisted as he said sadly, "I heard a noise and turned around. You are indeed master of these things. Can I be your helper? I too have some power. I will help the new human beings that are to come.

"You see, I can cure sickness, help interpret dreams, and control the mighty winds. Men and women looking like me will continue to assist others in the ages to come. Wearing a face carved in my likeness, blessed by sacred tobacco, my helpers will drive diseases before them into the winds. I will always listen when your people burn tobacco and pray to me for help."

Hawennihyoh agreed. "I will accept your help and I will even increase your power so you can better assist me in watching over the people who will come soon. You will have as members of your sacred society all who have been cured from sickness by your breath in the ceremony. They will be Doorkeepers of the Dance."

And so it was.

The Creation of the League

The myth of the founding of the Iroquois League, or Confederacy, which exists in many different versions, is one of the great stories of the world. It uses image and metaphor to explain the meaning of a new political order, one that deeply influenced the writing of the Constitution of the United States. No one knows just when the various Iroquois tribes banded together against the rest of the world, to live in peace from one another's raids, but it probably happened one or two centuries before Europeans reached the New World. Judging from the following story, and others related to it, the years before this agreement must have been periods of severe strife. Those were times when the different Iroquois tribes warred against one another and practiced cannibalism against their enemies. The agreement ended cannibalism among the tribes of the League and gave them a political union unlike any other in North America.

The metaphor of the longhouse became a powerful symbol of this union, for the longhouse sheltered the entire League. Just as the domestic longhouse was a strong shelter for the families it housed, the political longhouse sheltered the tribes. It stretched symbolically from the Eastern Door at the Hudson River, which was guarded by the Mohawks, to the Western Door guarded by the Seneca. The tribal chiefs were thought of as the posts of the longhouse; clan leaders were the braces that held these posts upright. Each tribe kept its own fire on the Iroquois trail, which stretched along the central aisle of the protecting political longhouse. The Onondagas, who lived in the middle, were considered "keepers of the fire." They hosted the meetings of the grand councils of the Iroquois, when all the tribes met in the Onondaga council house.

Long ago, in the time before recorded history, the Iroquois people held many great councils, but each one somehow failed. The evil wizard and tyrant Atotarho mysteriously prevented the chiefs from transacting any business.

Even though the chiefs of the people tried to exclude him from the councils by holding secret sessions, he always learned about the meetings from his many spies and appeared anyway. One time, in desperation, the chiefs chose a secret place to assemble, far away from their usual council fires. As before, Atotarho learned of the meeting from his spies. When the time came for the gathering, which had been set on the shores of a lake, Atotarho arrived there first.

He placed himself at the edge of the lake facing the water, silently waiting for the others, his head bowed deep in thought. He knew that most of the chiefs and their supporters would come across the lake by canoe. After a while the others began to arrive. Atotarho waited, unnoticed by the gathering crowd. Finally, when many were still out on the lake in heavily loaded canoes, Atotarho pulled himself up to his full height, surprising those around him. He called out in a loud voice, "A great storm is approaching. Hurry and reach shore or you are all doomed to die."

Those on the shore gasped with sorrow as they watched what happened next. No sooner were the words out of his mouth than fierce winds began to blow. The cries of fear and suffering resounded across the lake as the people fought the high waves and wind. All those who were still trying to reach shore perished in the storm.

The chiefs who were left murmured against Atotarho, feeling sure that he had caused the deaths of many good people. Yet they could do nothing but grumble to themselves for fear that Atotarho would strike them down. His spies and assassins were everywhere.

Again the chiefs called a secret council, this time near the lodge of the great chief Hayenwatha. Once again when the delegations arrived, they found Atotarho already there. Everyone wondered what horrible thing this powerful wizard, whose vengeance was boundless and who followed no rules of decent behavior, would do this time.

Hayenwatha's pregnant daughter went into the forest to gather wood for her fire. Upon seeing her alone, Atotarho shouted to all the people. "Look up, something is flying down to earth!" Crowds of people came rushing from camp to see a creature hurtling toward Hayenwatha's daughter. The crowd was so great, and the people so heedless of where they were running, that they ran right over the great chief's daughter, trampling her and her unborn child.

Hayenwatha wailed in grief as he saw his beautiful daughter fall among the rushing people. "Atotarho first caused two of my children to drown in the lake. Now he has taken from me my last child, and her child-to-be. They are all gone, destroyed by Atotarho." Bent in sorrow, Hayenwatha announced, "I must leave this evil place. I will split the sky. I will go south."

Crossing a great mountain, Hayenwatha eventually came to a lake on which many ducks floated. He called out to the ducks, "Birds who float on the surface of the lake, help me. Take up all the water so I may reach the bottom of the lake."

The ducks immediately flew up with all the water, leaving the lake empty. Hayenwatha walked through the mud a short way and dug into the bottom. There he found a quantity of wampum, which he placed in the pouch at his side.

With the wampum at his side, Hayenwatha turned east. As he walked, he gave names to many of the places he visited. He saw many moons grow large and wane before he came to a lodge. The owner invited him in, saying, "Why do you wander, seemingly without purpose, for you are clearly a noble man, worthy of great things?" The speaker was Deganawidah, wise in the ways of all things.

Hayenwatha answered him sorrowfully. "Atotarho, the mad one, has destroyed my three children and my unborn grandchild and left me in grief. His rage threatens us all. We must subdue him, but I know not how to proceed. He no longer has the mind of a human being."

"Where does Atotarho live?" asked Deganawidah.

"They say, in a lodge to the west and north from which smoke rises until it touches the sky. They say he has grown misshapen with his evil."

Deganawidah replied, "Let us call the other chiefs together. They may have wisdom to share about this matter."

At the council, the chiefs decided to meet with Atotarho as a group.

Deganawidah, who had called the council, agreed. "First we must prepare ourselves. We must be strong in mind and purpose to defeat Atotarho. If you are ready, then show your wampum strings.

No one could produce even so much as a single quahog shell, the one used to make wampum. They began to string ordinary shells together to symbolize twelve themes that they would use to change Atotarho's mind.

Then Deganawidah turned to Hayenwatha, who was at his side. "My friend, what can you contribute that will help us in our time of need?"

Hayenwatha reached into his pouch and drew out the thirteen strings of wampum he had earlier dug from the mud of the lake.

Deganawidah said, "We see that Hayenwatha has great power. With these strings of wampum our préparation can begin. Each represents a theme of wisdom and a law that we may use to straighten Atotarho's twisted mind. Let us now sing the Six Songs in thanks." Ever since that time, these songs have been sung for the common good.

Afterward Deganawidah asked for volunteers willing to search out Atotarho's dwelling. He selected a pair, two young men of strong purpose and upright mind. They transformed themselves into crows so they could fly far above the treetops and scan the horizon for any sign of smoke. Soon, far in the distance, they caught sight of a column of smoke rising above the treetops. They landed near the lodge and, taking back their human shape, walked through the clearing to the dwelling.

It was not Atotarho's lodge, but, upon hearing their errand, the owner, called The Great Tree because of his steadfastness and strength, said, "I will be like a massive tree trunk, lying across Deganawidah's path. Should he try to pass by, he will have to take me with him to rid the world of Atotarho's evil power. On your return, please stop and tell me what you find."

That night the two left, again assuming the form of crows. After searching

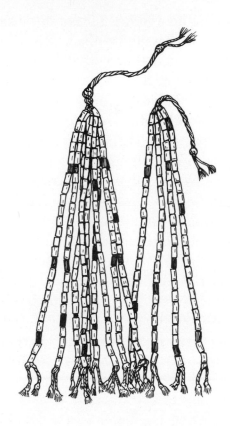

long and hard in all directions for signs of Atotarho, they eventually sighted a thick column of smoke snaking from the treetops high into the sky. Landing, and taking back their human form, they walked into the longhouse that was the source of the smoke.

"Is this the house of Atotarho?" they asked, in a loud voice.

"Hush, hush," warned several bystanders. "In this house, no one must speak above a whisper."

The crowd of silent people then parted just enough for the spies to see Atotarho himself. What they saw left them speechless with fear and disgust. Atotarho's evil nature had turned upon him and deformed his body. In place of hair, the wizard had developed a head of hissing serpents. His hands had become turtle's feet, his feet the claws of a bear. His body was folded over with many layers of fat. He was truly a monster.

Having seen enough, the two spies quickly left the place and took to the air. They were glad to be on their way home again, away from the misshapen being they had just seen. As they flew back to the council, they stopped off to report to the man called The Great Tree, the chief who a short time earlier had been their host. While there, they related to him all they had seen. He repeated his earlier boast. "Tell Deganawidah, I will be like a massive tree trunk, lying across his path. Should he try to pass by, he will have to take me with him to rid the world of Atotarho's evil power."

Home they flew, straight and true. When they arrived at the council and told all they had seen, Deganawidah said, "He has grown worse. We must all visit Atotarho in his lodge. We will try to restore his mind to its former self. On the way we will stop at the lodge of The Great Tree and we will say to him, "Work together with us to restore the mind of Atotarho to health."

They started right away, but stopped and rested at The Great Tree's lodge. The next morning after a short journey, they came to the edge of the woods where the forest and undergrowth grew thick. There they lit a fire and met in council with other chiefs who lived near the one with the twisted mind. After greeting each other, they sang the Six Songs. Atotarho, in his lodge, heard the singing. As he listened, a wonderful change came over him. For the first time in many years, his heart warmed and he felt pleasure at the singing.

After planning their next steps, the chiefs carried the thirteen wampum strings to Atotarho's lodge. Deganawidah was their spokesman. "You see before you Hayenwatha who came to my house in great trouble. Is this Atotarho's lodge?" The occupants were horrified by the sound of his voice, which boomed forth in the quiet lodge. "Shh, shh," they warned. "You must not speak so loud," and pointed toward the center, where Atotarho sat, his head covered with hissing snakes, his hands like turtle claws, and feet like bear claws.

Deganawidah was unafraid, and only spoke more forcefully. "We seek Atotarho. Chiefs, unwrap your themes that represent the law."

Thirteen chiefs responded quickly and took the thirteen wampum strings from Hayenwatha's pouch and laid them across a horizontal rod. Led by Deganawidah, they again sang the Six Songs. "You see before you the chiefs of the five nations. With the law that is represented by these strings of wampum, we are much stronger than Atotarho."

Atotarho listened attentively and then raised his misshapen head, which the people in his lodge had never seen him do.

"I am pleased by the singing of the Six Songs," he said. "They stir my heart."

Deganawidah spoke to the misshapen one in front of him. "We seek the great chief Atotarho. The mind now in his body is not the mind of a human being. We intend to reconstruct and reform his mind." Then Deganawidah sang a song while holding in his hand one of the lengths of wampum. All could see that Atotarho's mind was changing, for his face assumed a peaceful, benevolent expression.

"We must now straighten out your body and make it more natural," said Deganawidah. As he passed his hand over Atotarho's feet, they changed from bear's claws to human feet. Deganawidah delivered another string of wampum. Continuing with the rest of Atotarho's body, Deganawidah and the other chiefs restored all his features to their natural, human shape.

When they had finished restoring Atotarho, Hayenwatha and Deganawidah said, "We have restored Atotarho to his former self. The threat of great evil from this man has faded away. Now we can begin to bring peace to the Iroquois nations. Let us work to unite all tribes under laws that will ensure peace and tranquility."

The other chiefs nodded their agreement. Deganawidah continued, addressing the assembly in the great metaphors of the Iroquois Nation. "By bringing forth the Law that allowed us to restore Atotarho to his former self, we have torn up a great tree and made a great hole in the earth. At the bottom of this hole runs a stream, swift and deep. We have cast into this hole all the causes for further strife among us, so the stream could carry them away. Then we returned the tree to its place, where it shades the Iroquois nations.

"So long as we give our allegiance to it, the Law represented by this Tree of Peace will govern our land. The tree has sprouted a Great White Root that extends toward the setting sun; another extends toward the rising sun. A third goes south, splitting the sky; a fourth extends in the direction of the star that never moves. These are the Roots of the Law that we have made.

"An eagle that sees far sits atop the Tree of Peace keeping lookout in all directions with eyesight stronger than any other being. Should this bird see death and destruction approaching, he shall warn us in time for us to take action.

"We will light council fires to remind us of the Law that extends over us like a great longhouse, protecting us in all directions, east, south, west, north. We will kindle a fire for all nations so they may enjoy the benefits of the protection afforded by the Extended House we have now created."

Thus did Deganawidah speak, and all who listened agreed to keep the Law. When he had completed the work of founding the Extended House, which became the League of the Iroquois, Deganawidah spoke once more: "I have come to the end of my labors. Hayenwatha and you others must carry on the work we have started here." After Deganawidah passed one time through the Extended House he had founded, he came to the end of his life.

> How are we to understand this story? Deganawidah and Ha-yenwatha are the two mythical heroes who brought the long-house peace to the tribes. Each has different strengths. Deganawidah, who appears mysteriously midway through this version of the story, leads the move toward the League. Ha-yenwatha, also a great chief, is unable to act by himself against Atotarho until he meets Deganawidah.
>
> Atotarho symbolizes the many difficulties that prevented political unity. The severe storms he causes disrupt Iroquois life and destroy the proper order of society. Atotarho himself is outside the bounds of human society. His misshapen body reflects how fully his mind had become twisted.
>
> By banding together, Deganawidah and Hayenwatha, with the other chiefs, are able to redeem the evil Atotarho and reconstruct his mind. The edge of the woods, where Atotarho lived, represents his wildness and unpredictability. The fire

that the chiefs kindle symbolizes the council fire that will serve to help bind the nations together. The Six Songs, which alter Atotarho's mind and gladden his heart, probably represent the six nations of the Iroquois.

In some versions of the myth, Deganawidah *invents* wampum. In this one, it is Hayenwatha who *finds* wampum, but it is Deganawidah who gives wampum its special meaning. The Iroquois generally used wampum, which was made of shell beads sewn together, to send messages and to seal political agreements, for an exchange of wampum bound the speakers to any agreements they made. Words "talked into" wampum had to be the truth, for otherwise wampum would have quickly lost its ability to help memory, bind treaties, or send messages. Even today, the patterns sewn into wampum serve as reminders of historical and ceremonial events. Wampum still maintains an important role in Iroquois ritual. It is used in the Condolence Ceremony, which in Iroquois belief was invented by Deganawidah and first used to comfort Hayenwatha's grief.

The Tree of Peace, with roots that extend to the four directions, and a trunk that stretches from below Earth to the skies above, symbolizes the unity of the Iroquois League and its close connection with the cosmos. It also reflects greatness of size and strength. Like the longhouse that symbolizes the League, the Tree of Peace stretches above the Iroquois Nation and shelters the people.

2 A Gift of the Gods

The Navajo Hogan

To Navajo who keep their traditional ways, the world is sacred; and all things in it, whether people, animals, plants, or mountains, have their proper place. In the Navajo view, each person helps maintain the balance of the world by living in harmony with others and with his surroundings. Even the traditional Navajo house, the hogan, takes part in the balance of the world when it is properly made and aligned with the sky. Whether it serves as a dwelling or as a religious structure, the Navajo hogan is a sacred building, its plan ordained by the gods.

The Navajo live in a land of wide open horizons and long vistas. Especially in the summer, large puffy clouds rise above the mountains and sail through crisp blue skies, promising rain that rarely arrives in this high desert land. The rugged sandstone mesas provide a pleasing backdrop of pink, red, orange, buff, and gray. Dark green piñon pine and juniper dot a landscape covered mostly with sagebrush and rabbit bush.

Some Navajo have moved into cities and towns in Arizona, New Mexico, or Utah in or near the Navajo Reservation. Most, though, still live in small family settlements along one of the many miles of dirt roads that crisscross the Reservation. Many Navajo make a meager living by growing corn and other crops and by raising sheep and cattle.

The Emergence

Before people can build homes and sacred structures, they must have a land in which to live. According to the Navajo's traditional stories, in the beginning before they emerged to this present world, the people passed through either four or twelve underworlds. The *Dineh*, which means "The People" in the Navajo language, tried to live in each successive world, but found instead that they faced terrible hardships and privations. The *Dineh* could not live in these lower worlds. In the following story, the *Dineh* climbed through four successive worlds to reach this one.

The First World was like an island floating in a thick, watery mist. It was black as black wool. First Man was formed in the east, where the black cloud and the white cloud met. First Woman arose in the west, where the blue and yellow clouds met. There was no sun or moon in the First World, and it was so small that eventually the people quarreled. Seeking a better life, they climbed up out of the First World to the Second World, which was blue. Life was miserable in the Blue World, too, for the Swallow People, who lived there already, fought with the people who came up from the First World.

The people then looked for a way through the sky to the Third, or Yellow, World. Bluebird was the first to find the way to the Yellow World, which had six mountains and two rivers. One of the rivers flowed from north to south; the other flowed from east to west. The rest of the people soon followed Bluebird.

After they had surveyed the boundaries of the Third World, which were much larger than the two previous worlds, First Man brought the people together and taught them how to grow white corn. First Woman taught them to grow yellow corn. After a while, First Woman and First Man quarreled and all the women and men decided to live apart. After a short time, they found that neither group could do without the help of the other, so the men and women agreed to live together again as they still do today.

They were happy for a time, but eventually First Woman grew tired of their monotonous life. "Coyote, I have suffered many things in my life. I have a plan. Bring me the two pretty children of the Water Monster." Coyote traveled across the rainbow and entered the home of the Water Monster. He grabbed her children and made off, hiding them in his big coat.

Soon afterward, the people began to notice a great flood that arose on all sides of them. Only Coyote and First Woman knew the cause, but they kept silent even though the people began to cry that they would drown and die in the Third World. First Man brought everyone together again and climbed to the top of the highest of the six mountains. The water continued to rise steadily and followed them right on up. First Man planted the large Male Reed that Turquoise Boy, one of the First People who lived in the east, had brought him. He asked White Shell Girl, who lived in the west, to bring the Female Reed she had with her.

Everyone blew on the Male Reed and caused it to grow larger and larger. Eventually, the reed pierced the sky.

Yet when they tried to climb through the reed, they found it blocked. What could they do? The water still followed them as they climbed. Woodpecker stepped forward and drilled out the reed. They climbed into the Fourth World just ahead of the water.

The Fourth World was not a very large place, and the rising water followed them. Everyone was very frightened. The water also brought Water Monster. Lightning flashed from her two horns. She looked fierce indeed!

First Man said, "Why have you caused this flood? Why did you follow us into this world?" Water Monster remained silent. Then Coyote opened his coat and pulled out the two babies. "Perhaps this is why."

Turquoise Boy filled a basket with turquoise and on top he placed four kinds of pollen. Coyote took the basket and placed it between the horns of Water Monster as an offering. "I will give you back your male child. He shall be known as Male Rain, and he will bring thunder and lightning. The female child I will keep. She will be the gentle Female Rain that moistens the earth and helps plants to grow tall and strong." Water Monster disappeared into the flood, taking the water with her.

Fourth World was too small, and the waters had soaked the soil so it would not grow corn. First Man took the Female Reed White Shell Girl had given him in the Third World and planted it. Soon it grew large, and rose right up to the sky. Yet, when it pierced the sky, water began to drip through. This frightened Badger, who had offered to be the first to climb into the next world.

Locust came to everyone's rescue. "I come from the earth itself. I will climb into the next world through the mud and water above." Before he began his climb, Locust made a sacred headband of reed, and placed two arrows on it. With this and the help of all the others, Locust climbed through to the Fifth World. When he looked out across the water, he saw a large water bird headed toward him.

"Why have you come?" asked the bird. "This is not your world." Then, in a display of his power, the bird took an arrow and passed it into his mouth and through his body.

Locust laughed. "Why don't you do something useful, and take the water away? I don't plan to leave this world." Then Locust took the two arrows he had brought with him and passed them through his body, between his shell and his heart. He so impressed the bird with his sacred power that the bird did just what he was asked and took the water to the east.

Locust performed the same feat before the blue water bird from the south, the yellow water bird from the west, and the white water bird from the north. When the water birds had all left, Locust was standing on muddy land. He climbed back down to the world below and told the people of his encounter with the water birds. "The people of the Fifth World are powerful. It took all the power I had to send them away. The Fifth World is still wet and muddy, but the deep water has been taken away."

First Man thanked him and then gathered chips of turquoise as an offering to the five Chiefs of the Winds, who lived above the Fifth World. They sent strong winds to dry the Fifth World and make it habitable. Then First Man and First Woman led everyone to this world.

First Hogan: A Gift of the Gods

This myth, which is part of the creation story of the Navajo, tells the story of the First Hogan, the Planning Hogan. It conveys an impression of the First Hogan as a shelter of great beauty, fit for the task of planning the creation of the world. Every hogan built today reflects this First Hogan. The Navajo hold the hogan as a model, or representation, of the cosmos. Each major supporting log of the hogan belongs to one of the gods of the four directions.

When the First People, or Holy People, emerged from the four underworlds, they found a barren earth; neither plants nor mountains, nor even sun, moon, and stars, existed. From the underworld they had brought nothing — no food, clothing, or shelter. Before they could live in this new world, they first had to learn how to grow plants for food. They also needed to mold the earth and make it livable. First Man and First Woman talked over their circumstances. The two agreed that before they could do anything else they needed a home and a place in which to meet with the other Holy People to plan the order of the world. So, right where they emerged, before making any plans, they built the hogan. Everyone helped.

First Man began by digging a shallow pit that was to be the floor of the hogan. From Eagle he learned to make it round like the face of the sun. Gathering three large forked poles and two smaller ones, all made of precious stones, he placed them in the four directions. First Man started at the south corner. After digging a hole just outside the floor of the hogan, he placed the large end of the turquoise pole into the ground, and leaned the pole inward. For the west pole, First Man selected one made of abalone, and leaned its fork against the south turquoise pole. The remaining large pole, which was made of jet, he placed on the north side and leaned it against the first two. The two smaller poles of white shell he carefully planted at the east, to serve as an entranceway.

Beaver gave First Man and First Woman smaller logs to make a framework for the walls. Swallow offered adobe and straw to fill in the walls and floors. First Man and First Woman then covered the hogan with sunbeams and rainbows, which in those days were pliable coverings that could be used as blankets. The two sheets of rainbow they laid from north to south. Then, working from east to west, they placed sunbeams over the rainbows.

To bless their hogan, First Woman ground the corn she had carried up from the previous world and gave it to First Man. He entered the hogan, placing a pinch of cornmeal on each of the jeweled logs, East, South, West, and North. He said, "May our home be sacred and beautiful, and may our days be beautiful and plenty."

On the floor of the newly built hogan, First Man and First Woman spread a layered rug of jet, abalone, turquoise, and white shell. Then they made a curtain for the doorway from the dawn, from skyblue, and from evening twilight and darkness. They arranged the white dawn curtain so it faced the white shell rug. Finally, after bringing all their belongings into the First Hogan, the Holy People sang one of the songs that today accompany the building of hogans.

Along below the east, Earth's pole I first lean into position.
As I plan for it it drops, as I speak to it it drops, now it
    listens to me as it drops, it yields to my wish as it drops.
Long life drops, happiness drops into position, *ni yo o.*

Along below the south, Mountain Woman's pole I next lean in
    position.
As I plan for it it drops, as I speak to it it drops, now it
    listens to me as it drops, it yields to my wish as it drops,
Long life drops, happiness drops into position, *ni yo o.*

Along below the west, Water Woman's pole I lean between in
    position.
As I plan for it it drops, as I speak to it it drops, now it
    listens to me as it drops, it yields to my wish as it drops,
Long life drops, happiness drops into position, *ni yo o.*

Along below the north, Corn Woman's pole I lean my last in
    position.
As I plan for it it drops, as I speak to it it drops, now it
    listens to me as it drops, it yields to my wish as it drops,
Long life drops, happiness drops into position, *ni yo o.*

First Man and First Woman stepped back to look at their planning hogan and saw that it was beautiful. Then they entered and turned to other tasks of creation.

The hogan described in this myth is called a five-pole hogan. It is the oldest style of hogan; two skilled builders can put it up in about a day. The five-pole hogan is considered to be a "male" hogan and is modeled after Fir Mountain, which is one of the six Navajo sacred mountains. Today, it is more common to see a style of hogan having a more rounded roof. This "female" hogan, built of logs or ordinary wood framing, resembles the low, extended mesa that the Navajo call Mountain Around Which Traveling Was Done, because in the old days it took a long time to ride around it on a horse or in a wagon. These hogans can be much larger than the older, five-pole type and today often contain windows as well.

Most Navajo today live in rectangular gabled houses. However, many still maintain a hogan nearby, either for ceremonial purposes or to house older family members who feel more comfortable in the traditional hogan.

The Navajo people bless the newly built hogan with white cornmeal. The builder enters from the east and, moving as the sun does around to the south, he blesses first the east poles, then the south, west, and finally north pole.

The First Hogan was built round like the sun because the sun gives heat, light, and protection from evil. The hogan's single doorway faces east in order to be open to the kindly influences of the God of Dawn. Commonly, the hogan is oriented so the doorway faces in the direction of sunrise on the day of construction. When the Navajo enter the hogan, they follow a "sunwise course," around to the left, which mimics the sun's course through the sky from east, through south, to west and north. This means that to reach a point on the right side of the hogan, they must walk around the fireplace, or stove, which is generally placed near the center of the hogan.

The Sky Hogan

The Navajo consider the sky itself as a kind of hogan, providing shelter for the entire earth. The following story tells how the Holy People fashioned the sky in the pattern of the First Hogan.

In the First Hogan, First Man and First Woman planned for the time that was to come. They discussed how the people were to live and decided they had to have a sun to bring daytime light and heat to help plants grow. They also wanted a moon to guide travelers at night.

First Man and First Woman, helped by the others, laid out a beautiful buckskin. On it they placed a perfect circle of turquoise, which was larger than a man. Around the edge of this great turquoise disk they attached twelve eagle feathers and twelve feathers from the bird, Flicker. After marking the disk with eyes, a nose, and a mouth, they asked Fire God to heat it with his fire.

Below the turquoise disk that was to be the sun, they placed a perfect white shell, which would become the moon. First Man used his fire crystal to heat the moon, which was to give a lesser light. Turquoise Boy then stepped into the sun and, with his flute, moved the sun through the sky. White Shell Girl, likewise, stepped into the white shell and moved the moon. Together, Turquoise Boy and White Shell Girl made the seasons, the months, and the days.

After they had made the heavenly bodies, their next task was to make the sky. Again, the others who had come up from the underworld assembled to help. Stretching the blue sky above the earth, they gathered four large poles made of jewels. In the east, they planted a white shell pole in the earth, to hold up the eastern side of the sky. Taking a turquoise pole, they planted it in the south to support the southern sky. An abalone pole was placed in the west, and a jet one in the north. After they checked to see that the poles were firmly placed, they fashioned a hole in the sky and sealed it with water. Then, on the outer edge of the heavens, they made a border of a white ring, a blue ring, and a black ring. The Holy People made the rings to protect the sky so that no power anywhere, whether on the earth or above the earth, would be able to harm it. Finally, around each of the four posts they placed the colors white, blue, yellow, and black, in that order. The Holy People stepped back and saw that it was beautiful indeed.

3 Emergence from the Underworld

The Pueblo Kiva

The stone and adobe villages of the Southwest amazed the early Spanish explorers when they first rode north from Mexico in the sixteenth century. Seen from a distance, the clusters of rooms piled one atop another seemed to be just one more part of the multicolored sandstone mesas they were built upon. Yet, up close, these terraced structures were clearly the work of skilled architects and builders.

Francisco Vásquez de Coronado and his men called these Native Americans the Pueblo Indians because their villages resembled the *pueblos*, or towns, of the Spanish soldiers' homeland. In these villages, they found a peaceful people who lived in well-made stone or adobe houses and who had learned to prosper in the high desert.

The ancestors of the Pueblo people began to develop their villages over a thousand years ago. Today the tribes include the Hopi and the Zuni in Arizona and western New Mexico, and the eastern groups such as the Acoma, Isleta, Santa Clara, and Jemez near the Rio Grande. They live very differently from the Navajo, who settled some five hundred to seven hundred years ago in the same region, but who are not village dwellers. Although the different Pueblo groups speak several distinct languages, they have similar customs and a related body of mythology and folk stories. Traditionally, they have lived by farming and hunting. They raise a few sheep and cattle, the descendants of animals the Spanish brought with them four hundred years ago. However, raising corn, beans, squash, and melons is most important to them. The Southwest receives a lot of sun and very little rain each year, but the special farming techniques developed by the Pueblo farmers have enabled them to survive and prosper despite the harsh dry climate.

The Pueblo Indians have a rich ceremonial life, built around the desire for the growth of crops and respect for all living things. In this sun-drenched land, every little bit of rain is treasured. Especially during the growing season, prayers for rain play a major role in most Pueblo religious ceremonies.

The Pueblo people have a strong sense of place. Their world is bounded by mountains in all directions, and the mountains are the source of clouds and rain that bring water to the crops. The mountains also contain shrines to the sun and other deities — sacred places that help focus the prayers of the tribe for growth and well-being.

According to the Pueblo account of creation, their ancestors came to this world from an underworld several levels below this one. The Hopi and Zuni, for example, believe that humans started in the underworld and climbed through three levels to reach this, the fourth world. The Hopis often refer to the levels as houses. The four houses rest atop one another much as the houses do in a Pueblo village.

Finding the Center

According to this Zuni story, after climbing up from the worlds below, the people wandered about in the four directions in search of a place to settle and build permanent dwellings. Finally, after much dispute, and with the help of Water Strider, the tiny bug who lives on the surface of the water, they were able to find The Center, or The Middle Place. The Zuni consider the six directions, north, south, east, west, above, and below, to be sacred. Hence, it is appropriate that Water Strider, with his six legs, reached toward all six directions to find The Middle Place.

After emerging from the Underworld, through the place of emergence, which the Hopi call the *sipapu*, the men, women, and other beings scattered into groups, each group finding a place that suited it, declaring that its own home was The Center, or The Middle Place.

Each group complained that the others were in error and not living according to the rules given in the Underworld. There was no peace among the groups.

After much argument, they all decided to hold a great council and determine once and for all the location of The Middle Place. Someone suggested that they ask Water Strider to help them. "Water Strider, the one who skates on water, has great long legs that can extend in each of six directions to the outer edges."

Water Strider agreed to help. Some say that Water Strider was Sun Father in disguise. He grew larger, stretched his six legs, and lifted himself high above the ground, to the very heavens. He then pushed out his legs in all directions until they touched the waters to the north, west, south, and east at the edges of the world. One leg reached to the waters above in the northeast and one to the waters below in the southwest.

The leg that extended to the north touched the frigid water there and shrank back a little. Because the waters to the west were nearer than the others, he drew his leg back a little there as well. Then he gradually let his body settle back to the earth. "My heart and navel are resting on The Middle," he told them. "Here at the Center of Mother Earth you are to build your town."

The place Water Strider settled his body was the valley of Zuni, and there a town was built. Then, slowly, Water Strider drew in his long legs. Where he drew them in, he left trails radiating from Zuni in all six directions.

Zuni was built at the place Water Strider indicated — no one knowing that he had drawn two of his feet back, swerving a little to the south in settling his body. However, all were content with their new home. Peace was restored.

Sun Father's House

Sun Father is very important to the Pueblo people. Sun provides light for daily activities and heat for the plants. Sun's heat also helps form the summer clouds that hold the rain needed for crops. Thus it is not surprising that Sun Father plays a strong role in Pueblo ceremonies.

Traditional Pueblo people reckon the passage of time by the sun. Even today, when they, like other citizens, follow the everyday calendar, they still depend on a solar calendar to determine when to begin ceremonies or to plant crops. The village sunwatcher observes the slow yearly movement of the sun along the horizon from a sunwatching shrine or from a special place in the village. He knows that when the sun rises behind a certain mountain or deep notch on the horizon, it is time to begin preparations for a summer dance, or for the winter solstice ceremony in late December. Not only do the Pueblo people watch the horizon, they may also mark places on their interior walls on which the sun's rays fall through-windows on particular days. Thus their houses may become observatories for noting the passage of time.

One of the most important Pueblo stories takes place in the Beginning, before the earth was fully formed, when there were no mountains, streams, or rivers. The sun's light fell through a small hole in the wall of a house and caused a maiden to become pregnant.

In the Hopi version of the story, four days later, which for the Hopi is a sacred length of time, she gave birth to twin boys, Poqangwhoya and Palonqwhoya. In four more days these babies grew to be strong boys whose clowning behavior exasperated their mother, their grandmother, and the Hopi people. Nevertheless, these brave boys helped rid the earth of four terrible monsters.

The Twins wanted to know who their father was, and where he lived. They longed to see his house and have their father acknowledge them as his sons. Yet every time they asked, their Spider Grandmother avoided a direct answer, saying, "How should I know?" She was afraid they would try to visit Sun in his house. Still, like young people everywhere, they pestered her with questions: "Who is our father? Where does he live?"

Finally, she gave in and told them. "Your father is the sun, who lives far away to the east at the place of sunrise. But you must not try to visit him. He is very powerful. No one has come back from there alive."

The boys persisted. "We want to visit our father. When he learns who we are, surely he will give us many wonderful gifts. He might give us something to rid the earth of the terrible monsters that have been plaguing the people. Please help us. We want to leave right away."

In the end Spider Grandmother reluctantly agreed to help them, convinced they would go with or without her help. She rubbed them with a powerful root to protect them from danger and help them overcome obstacles. They hurried off in great excitement.

The Twins traveled far to the east, to the place of sunrise. Here there is a place where Sun's House can be entered only through a deep canyon in the sky. The canyon sides are very steep and they open and close like huge jaws, crushing anyone who tries to enter. Fierce guards control the canyon and admit no one.

The Twins chewed a root Spider Grandmother gave them, holding it in their mouths until they arrived at the entrance to the canyon. When the canyon jaws began to tremble and threatened to snap shut, the Twins spit the potion on both sides, and the canyon walls fell still.

They rushed through, still fearful that the walls would wake up and crush them. Their hearts were high as they reached the end of the canyon, for there was the doorway to Sun Father's house. But they grew fearful as they approached the doorway, for there before them were four dreadful guards — Lion, Bear, Rattlesnake, and Serpent — barring their way into the house. Approaching each guard in turn, they spurted more of the root Spider Grandmother had given them, saying, "Do not be angry, friend," and one by one the fearsome guards lay down quietly.

They stood in the entrance taking in the vast interior. Sun's house was like an enormous kiva and could be entered only from the top by a ladder. The only people they saw below them were many beautiful young women, busily working. These were Sun's daughters. Some were making pottery. Others were grinding corn or cooking *piki*, the delicious thin cornmeal cakes the Hopis make. Seeing the boys standing, looking down the hatch, one of Sun's daughters said, "Look there, who are those snotty-nosed boys? How did they get in here?"

Sun's wife looked up to see the two dirty little boys (the Twins were always dirty from playing so hard) standing there looking down. She invited them in. "Come on down the ladder," she said. As the boys climbed down, they saw in the middle of the room a large mound of turquoise with a huge abalone shell on top. "This must be the seat of Sun Father," they whispered to each other. Around this mound were many smaller ones for the wife and daughters to sit on.

Sun's wife asked them who they were, but the Twins only smiled and said nothing. She grew very angry with them. Sun's daughters then asked who they were. When the Twins still did not answer, the daughters said, "Fine. You sit here and be our brothers until our father comes home from his travels. Then we will know who you are."

Then the daughters changed their minds and decided to hide the Twins until Sun Father arrived. They placed them in The Place of Clouds, where they were covered with beautiful clouds of all colors.

After a time, the Twins heard a great bellowing as Sun returned from his daily journey from the east to the west and climbed into the house through a hatchway in the floor. After his daily trip, he always passed through the Below to enter his house.

No sooner had he taken his seat on the great mound of turquoise in the center of the house than he hollered, "Who is here? I smell strangers! Bring them to me."

When the Sun's daughters led them out from The Place of Clouds, the Twins ran toward Sun and cried out, "Sun Father, we are your sons."

"We'll see about that," said Sun, picking them up. Now Sun's house had a huge iron stove off to one side and always had a great fire going. Sun strode over to the stove, and, opening the door, he tossed both of them in and stoked up the fire till it roared. Then he opened up a little hole and poured in water to make steam. Great quantities of steam poured out of the stove as the water hissed and bubbled. After a time he opened the door and peered in. There were the boys, sitting in the middle of the hot stove playing a stick game with one of the pieces of firewood. "Brrr. Close the door," they complained. "You're letting in a cold draft."

Then Sun knew they were indeed his sons. When the Twins emerged, unscathed, laughing and dancing, Sun said, "You are surely my sons. I put you in the stove to make sure. I am glad to see you." Then he hugged them and washed them to make them beautiful.

"What can I give you for gifts?"

When the Twins told him of all the monsters on the earth that were troubling the Hopi people, and how they wanted to help, Sun gave them lightning. To the elder boy, Sun gave yellow lightning. To the younger he gave blue lightning. They were so happy that they danced around, holding their gifts tight. Then Sun instructed them in the use of their powerful new gifts.

The Twins stayed with Sun four nights. On the fifth morning, Sun took them with him. He carried the sun disk like a shield on his right arm. Carrying both boys, he took them with him on his daily sky-journey so they might see the whole world.

The First Kiva

The Acoma Indians live west of the Rio Grande in central New Mexico. Their traditional home is the top of a large mesa, where they have laid out their houses in neat rows. Although the Acoma return to their "Sky City" for ceremonial events, most now live in modern houses below the mesa.

In most Pueblo villages, the houses, which are made of stone and dirt like the earth, cluster around a central plaza, which is open to the sky. The form of the village always reminds the people of their connections with earth and sky. In earlier days, the people spent most of their days out of doors, making pottery and tools or preparing food.

The primary Pueblo sacred structure is the kiva, which is often located in the plaza near the center of the village. Each clan has its own kiva. According to Pueblo legend, when the people emerged from the worlds below, one of the first things they did was build a kiva in which to worship.

According to their origin myths, the Acoma people were descended from two sisters, Iatiku, the first born, and Nautsiti who was born later. After they had grown a bit, the sisters heard the voice of a female spirit whom they called Tsichtinako. She taught the girls how to speak and gave them gifts of seeds and images of all the animals there were to be in the world. Then Tsichtinako helped the girls climb from the underworld into this world and gave them instructions for planting corn and for praying to the creator of the world.

The story of the first kiva of the Acoma people reflects the importance of the four directions to the Acoma. The kiva described in this story is a kind of model of the world and represents its important features, such as the horizon, the Milky Way, the rainbow, and the four directions. What makes this story particularly interesting and demonstrates its age is that all of the kivas in use today are rectangular. The Acoma have not used circular kivas for centuries, though their ancestors, the Anasazi, who lived throughout the Four Corners area of the Southwest, built circular kivas.

Iatiku, the first born, and Nautsiti, her sister, came up from the darkness of the underworld through the *sipapu* into the light of this world. They climbed up on the trunks of four trees that Tsichtinako had instructed them to plant in the underworld. Tsichtinako told them, "You will find the seeds of four kinds of pine tree in your baskets. Each one comes from one of the four directions. Plant these seeds and they will grow into trees that will help you reach the light."

Iatiku picked the Corn Clan as her clan because the first seeds she was given were of corn. Nautsiti chose the Sun Clan, for she wanted to see the sun. After the first kachinas, the masked dancers, appeared to the people, Iatiku realized that they had no sacred house for the kachinas to live in. Addressing the people she said, "The kiva must be built in a certain way. It is to represent the *sipapu*, where we came up." She first directed the people to dig a deep round hole in the ground. Next, she instructed them to make offerings of four jewels. In the north under the foundation they placed yellow turquoise; in the west, blue turquoise. For the south, they selected red turquoise, and in the east they placed white turquoise. They also planted prayer sticks in each of the four directions along with the jewels so the foundation would stay strong and never give way.

Then Iatiku told the people to take four logs from the four directional trees to make a roof. After that, they covered the roof, leaving a hole for a ladder. After Oak Man dug a hole, the people made a ladder from the first four trees. The ladder, which they used to climb in and out of the kiva, stretched over the fireplace, so the fire would purify the people when they climbed up and down.

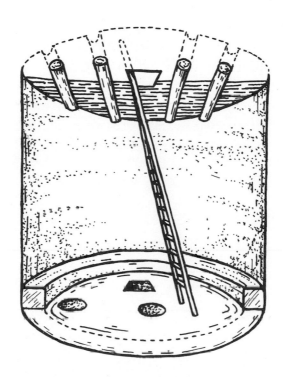

When the kiva was complete, all the people rested in the kiva and listened to Iatiku explain its meaning. She said, "The walls of the kiva surround us as the sky does, so when we are in the kiva we can remember the sky's beauty. The roof beams stretch across the kiva as the Milky Way stretches across the night sky. We built the kiva round to be like the sky where it meets the Earth. The ladder you built from the wood of the first four trees I call the rainbow because we never see the end of the rainbow. That is just like the trees of the underworld. We never saw where they touched the ground."

Then Iatiku gave them certain instructions about how to use the kiva. "Always enter the kiva facing the ladder. Whenever you enter or leave, you should never stop until you reach the bottom, for it will shorten your life. When you climb out of the kiva do not look back, because when my sister Nautsiti and I climbed up from the underworld to this world we did not stop or turn back.

"When you reach the bottom of the ladder in the kiva, you must always turn to the right to take your seat, and never to the left. Never take fire from the front of the fireplace and don't step into it. Never whistle in the kiva. When the kachinas come from the four directions, you must invite them into the kiva for our ceremonies. We have covered their seats with skins of bear and mountain lion." These were the rules Iatiku made for the people in those days.

4 Shade and Shelter
Mohave Houses

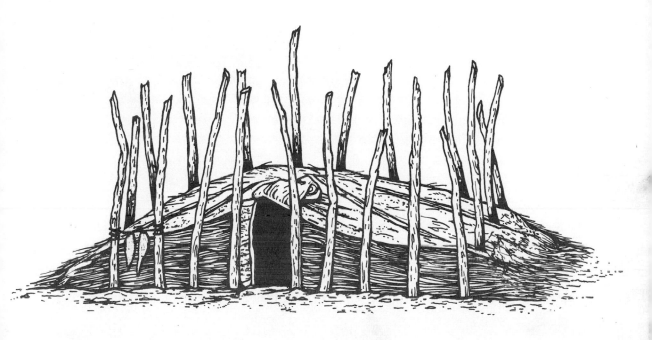

The Mohave Indians live just to the east of the Mohave Desert along the Colorado River, which separates Southern California and Arizona. It is an area of mild winters, extremely hot summers, and very little rain. In the lowlands along the river, water-loving trees like cottonwood and willow flourish. Away from the river and at a little higher elevation, mesquite trees are common. Still farther away on the mesas, even these small trees give way to desert cacti and creosote bushes. The mountains beyond are parched and nearly barren. In the last century, the Colorado flowed strong and free, flooding its banks in the spring. Today this part of the Colorado River is only a ghost of its former self. By the time it reaches the Gulf of

Mexico, about a hundred fifty miles south of Mohave country, the Colorado, tamed by dams and canals, is reduced to a mere trickle.

The Mohave were first seen by Europeans when the Spanish expedition of 1604 led by Juan de Oñate rode through the region. Then, and later when Euro-American settlers moved into the area, the Mohave lived in widely scattered settlements on the Colorado River floodplain. It is a harsh, unforgiving land requiring great skill and knowledge to survive and prosper. The Mohave were able to make a living in this demanding climate because of the spring floods, when the river brought torrents of water and fertile soil from the Rockies and deposited them in these broad lowlands. They located their houses on the highest ground, where the flooding waters would pass by them unharmed. Each spring, after the waters drew back from their fields, they would plant corn, tepary beans, pumpkins, and melons in the fertile soil. Following the spring floods, the hot summer sun quickly ripened crops and wild plants, bringing fresh food to humans and animals alike.

The men caught fish in the river and hunted small animals. The women gathered wild seeds from trees and plants along the river. From the desert they collected mesquite and screwbean pods, cactus fruit, and various plants and herbs.

As important as the Colorado was to the Mohave, they developed no true boats, but were excellent swimmers. If they needed to transport goods or children on the river, they would generally use a large pottery vessel, pushing it along as they swam. They often used log rafts to carry an entire family down river. The men were powerful runners and some could run across the desert as far as a hundred miles in a single day.

Dreaming, and the telling of dreams, was deeply important to the Mohave. A person's special talent and skills, or any successes in life, were thought to come from proper dreaming. For the Mohave, all dreams, many of which related to the beginnings of the world, had meaning. Their dreams kept the distant past always with them. A person's dreams were frequently discussed and interpreted, and could be used to foretell events. What they called "Great Dreams" bestowed great personal power and prestige. To a few people, Great Dreams gave the skill and power necessary to become shamans, chiefs, braves, war heroes, singers, and funeral orators.

In place of the complex religious rituals that most other tribes practiced, the Mohave emphasized the telling of their dreams and the singing of songs. A storyteller/singer might take an entire night to tell of the mythological events of the Beginning Time. Alternating songs with stories, the singer would describe events from those days, such as the deeds and travels of gods and animals. The longest Mohave myths tell the history of the tribe and may take all night to tell.

Mastamho Builds a Ramada

The oppressive heat that soon develops in early summer makes some sort of shelter from the sun a necessity. The Mohave developed open-sided ramadas, or shades, to protect them from the sun's fierce light. The roofs served double duty as drying racks for corn and other foods. In this dry climate, shade was often all that was needed in a place to rest or work. The following myth from the many stories of the Beginning Time tells how Mastamho, the younger of two brother gods,

showed the people how to build the first ramada. Nearby tribes
were often mentioned in the myths, as the Mohave traded,
worked, and sometimes fought with these close neighbors.

At first there was only the male Sky and the female Earth. They touched far in
the west, and from this union came the brothers Matavilya and Mastamho and
all humans and other beings. Matavilya led everyone upward to the place called
"house-post water," along the Colorado River. It was the center of the world, as
he determined by stretching his arms to the north, south, east, and west. There
he made the Great Dark House, a massive round house where the people would
dream Great Dreams. It was from dreams received here that the people would
derive all the power they would have while living.

The Great Dark House had four doors, one in each direction, but no one
could see it because in that early time, before the sun, moon, and stars were yet
made, it was utterly dark. Matavilya summoned everyone to the house, even
without speaking, and caused them to crawl around in the darkness to learn its
parts. They felt each doorway, each post, wall, and the roof, learning how it was
put together. Then he had the people sit at the southern door, while Matavilya
and Mastamho sat in the north door.

Soon after dreaming was given to the people in the Great Dark House,
Matavilya was killed. He was later cremated and the Great Dark House was
burned. The earth was still unformed and the people had no crafts, or skills.
They did not even know how to speak. Mastamho, the younger brother, was left
to lead and instruct the people.

Mastamho began his work by shaping the land — he made mountains, valleys, and the Colorado River. Then he made the sky and all the great sky
beings — the sun, moon, and stars. He divided the people into four groups —
Chemehuevi, Walapai, Yavapai, and Mohave — and gave them each a place
to live. He made springs in the four areas so the people would not thirst. In each
tribe's separate area, he took seeds and showed them how to plant and harvest.
He showed the people how to grind corn, how to make pottery, and how to use
tools. While he was doing these things, he taught them the words for everything
he was doing. He taught them how to speak, and how to understand each other.

"To each of you four tribes, I have given something," Mastamho said. "But for the Mohave, I have something else. I want to show you how to build a shade, a ramada."

Now in this early time, the ground was still wet, soft, and unformed. Mastamho looked around and saw Ant making a home underground. Ant chewed the wet earth to make a hole and spat the sand in a heap at the entrance to dry. Mastamho felt the sand and knew that this dry spot would be a good place to build a ramada.

"Ant, make dry ground for a ramada," Mastamho said. Ant did as he was asked. When he finished, there was a huge pile of dry sand.

Again Mastamho looked around. He saw Wasp busy kicking and throwing dirt out of his way as he burrowed. That gave Mastamho an idea.

He had the people pace out the area for the ramada and mark the postholes. Then he called Ant and Wasp. "Ant," he said, "I want you to dig the holes and set the support posts in them. Wasp, I want you to move the sand further away as Ant digs, and level the ground."

To the people Mastamho said, "Call the posts *avulypo*. Say it, say *avulypo*." The people practiced saying *avulypo*.

Mastamho instructed the people to cut roof supports and lay them across the upright posts. "Call the roof support beams *igumnau*," he told them. The people all said *igumnau*.

"Now take poles and lay them across the support beams. They are called *avatsutara*. Thatching, which you cut from the plants near the river, you should use to lay across the roof supports. It is called *avatsusive* (arrowweed)." The people repeated all these words as they worked.

"Cover the thatching with willow and call it *avanyuts*," he told them.

Then Mastamho turned to the Mohave and said, "Now you have a shade. It will protect you from the heat of the sun during the day. If it should rain, it will protect you then as well." The Mohave people entered the shade and sat down. None of the other tribes sat under the shade. The Chemehuevi sat outside just to the west. The Walapai sat on the northeast and the Yavapai to the southeast.

The Winter House

The desert winters are generally cold enough that the Mohave need more shelter than a ramada can provide. The Mohave built their winter houses by digging a shallow pit and placing a square of four posts in the sand to support the central part of the roof. Poles extended out from those to other, shorter posts on the periphery. The roof, which sloped down from the center nearly to the earth on three sides, was made of willow poles. It was thatched with arrowweed, and covered with a thick layer of mud. The wall containing the doorway was also covered with mud. In good weather, the Mohave spent much of their social time on the rooftop, which they reached by walking up the sloping sides. The entrance opened to the east and served both as a doorway and as a smoke hole. Some of these houses were large enough to accommodate several families. In the myth of Mastamho's deeds in creating the world, after he demonstrates how to build a ramada, Mastamho then proceeds to build a winter house.

After Mastamho had built the shade for the people and told the Mohave that it was good, he turned and said to the people, "Now I will build a house."

"The shade is good," he continued, "and it is useful most of the year. But it is not good always to sit under the ramada."

Mastamho looked around to be sure that the people were listening. Everyone was silent and all eyes were on him. Satisfied, he continued.

"You know nothing about the winter. You only know that the ramada keeps the summer sun away. In the winter the air feels cold, the rains fall, and the wind blows. The ramada will not protect you from the cold or the wind or the rain, but a house will keep you warm and dry."

Again Mastamho turned to Ant and Wasp. "Build another framework exactly as before." Ant and Wasp dug the postholes, smoothed the earth, and put the posts in place.

As before, Mastamho told the people to say the words as they placed the posts, and put the roof supports, the roof poles, thatching, and willow in place. They repeated the words as they worked.

"Now this time," said Mastamho, "enclose three sides of the house with willow." The people wove long willow branches between the upright posts to make walls.

When they were finished, Mastamho told the Mohave to heap sand on the roof and against the walls to keep out the rain and winds. "Call the sand *avataive.*"

Then Mastamho said to the people, "When the house is finished, you must make a fourth wall for the door. I will tell you what to do."

Following his instructions, the people again wove willow between the house posts in order to create a wall for the door. Then they took bark from dead cottonwood trees and wove it to make a large mat. This mat they tied to a pole. When they had hung the door, Mastamho named it *avapete.*

Now Mastamho was thinking of the time that he must leave the people. He named the Ant and Wasp helpers and told the people that the helpers would appear to them in dreams. Mastamho said, "I must go soon and you will see me no more except in dreams. I will not die like Matavilya, but I will become a bird and fly away. The people will dream and see me. I will give them power."

Before he left, Mastamho gave the people food and taught them how to plant. He gave them sunset to mark the time between day and night. Sunset, he told them, is the time to come into the house to be warmed by the fire.

"Mountains will always be with you, but I cannot be with you always. Night and day are here always, and so is sunset."

Then Mastamho leaned against the doorway of the house. "Go to sleep now, it is night," he said. "I have taught you enough for today. Tomorrow I will speak to you again."

After all his work was complete, Mastamho transformed himself into an eagle, so he would not be far away from the people. He said, "Through your dreams I will always be with you. I will come to you and teach you what you need to know to live a good and prosperous life."

5 Sun's Crystal House

California House Myths

The land that is now the state of California was once home to more than sixty distinct Native American groups. Its highly varied topography, climate, and food resources made possible the development of a number of complex societies. Food production tied them closely to both the land and the water. Most California Indians lived by hunting, fishing, and gathering. The coastal peoples derived much of their food from the ocean. Those who lived along the rivers or lakes ate freshwater fish and plants. Some of the groups that lived inland on the eastern California deserts hunted animals and gathered plants and seeds. Others, like the Mohave, Pima, or Papago further east, gathered plants and grew such crops as corn, beans, and squash.

California groups were organized in small groups called tribelets, smaller than a tribe but having a distinct language and culture. Like their neighbors to the north along the Pacific Coast, or those in the deserts of the Southwest, long before the arrival of Europeans, the California Indians had learned how to gather, process, and prepare many kinds of foods. They had also become highly accomplished artisans, builders, politicians, and storytellers.

Sun's Crystal House (Chumash)

Remarkably little is known of the history of the Chumash, who once lived along the coast and on the islands near the modern city of Santa Barbara. From their first contact with the Spanish in 1542 to their eventual disappearance three centuries later, the Chumash were friendly and helpful. Unfortunately, this eventually proved their undoing. Spanish missionaries worked hard converting them to Christianity and making the Chumash and the neighboring tribes into farmers and workers for the benefit of the Spanish. By crowding them into compounds near the missions, the Spanish inadvertently exposed them to smallpox, measles, and other European diseases to which Native Americans had no resistance. By the end of the nineteenth century, the Chumash and their culture had nearly vanished.

What little anthropologists have been able to learn of the Chumash shows that they had an advanced culture. The mild climate of Southern California and the abundance of food made life especially comfortable for these oceanside dwellers. They lived in well-organized villages that might number a thousand or more inhabitants. The Chumash built fine, planked seagoing canoes and other watercraft for fishing; wove intricate baskets; and made excellent stone and bone tools. They had a detailed knowledge of the skies and closely observed the motions of the sun and stars. This information helped them know when to gather certain foods or when to hold important religious ceremonies.

The early Spanish explorers thought the Chumash houses looked like large half-oranges laid on the ground. They were built from a circular framework of long willow poles about as thick as a man's arm. Each pole was sunk a foot or more into the earth, bent over, and lashed to its opposite across the circle to form a large, open dome. The builders then lashed smaller poles horizontally around the dome in such a way that they formed pairs opposite each other, one inside and one outside. Before the house was covered with thatch, it looked like a loosely woven basket turned upside down. The thatch was made either of reeds called tule (pronounced too-lee), or of grasses. It was fastened between the inside and outside horizontal poles, and layered to shed the rain.

Although the thatch shed rain and protected from all but the fiercest winds, it was no match for the mischief of little boys. One anthropologist was told of the time that a woman was sitting inside her house with her back against the wall. Two playful boys outside stuck a sharp stick through the thatch

Sun the whole way back to Sun's crystal house, asserting that he knew very well how to carry the torch. Finally, when they were nearly at the door, Coyote stopped and said, "Well, if that's the way you're going to treat me, I won't stay at your house."

Coyote walked off by himself. He decided he would leave the sky country and go back to earth. But first he had to find the golden eagle, Slo'w. When he finally found him, Slo'w paid Coyote no attention. He just kept watching the world below. It was Slo'w's job to keep the upper world in place. Every once in a while, when he gets tired, Slo'w stretches his wings a bit and causes the moon to grow dimmer. We see this every month in the phases of the moon. Sometimes he covers the moon entirely and causes an eclipse.

Coyote kept talking, saying anything to get Slo'w to pay attention and speak to him. "There sure are a lot of bones around here. You're a bad man. Why, how do I know you haven't eaten my wife while I've been up here visiting Sun? How about helping me get back down to earth?"

Slo'w kept silent. Finally, after Coyote had badgered him for a long time, the big bird spoke testily. "I can't help you get back."

"Sure you can," said Coyote. "All you have to do is to stretch your wing toward earth and then I can run down it."

Slo'w was very skeptical, but he wanted very much to get rid of Coyote. "I will try," he said, as he stretched his wing downward, ever downward, toward earth.

Afraid that Slo'w would change his mind, Coyote immediately jumped on his wing and ran down as fast as he could. He ran a long time, and then, thinking that he must be almost to this world, he jumped off Slo'w's wing. But he was still far above earth. He tumbled through the air and hit the ground with a thud. Pieces of Coyote flew all over. He was as dead as a lump of rock.

When people heard Coyote hit the ground, everyone came out to see what had happened. There were parts of Coyote everywhere. Here was an ear. There was his tail. Somewhere else was one of his feet. Everyone helped to gather up the pieces and put him back together. As soon as they revived Coyote, he jumped up and ran around.

"Thank you everyone. I was just resting after my long and strenuous trip to the sky. Let me tell you all about it."

Coyote never would admit that he had died in the fall and had to be put back together by his friends. But now we know all about his journey to Sun's crystal house, because Coyote told us.

The Theft of Fire (Miwok)

Before 1848, when Euro-American explorers discovered gold in the rivers of Central California and started a rush to the region, the Miwok Indians lived comfortably on the productive lands east of the Sacramento and San Joaquin rivers. They hunted birds, animals, and insects, and gathered great quantities of plants, seeds, and nuts. Acorns were a favorite Miwok food and were stored in great basket-like granaries supported by thick posts.

The Miwok built several types of houses, depending on the season, the local climate, and the uses to which the houses were put. Simple thatched conical sun shelters were used in the summers, especially during camping trips. In the winter the Miwok lived in large circular buildings sunk partly in the earth, which were entered by a ladder through the roof. They also built small, conical, earth-covered sweathouses, and small brush huts for menstruating girls and women.

The assembly house was a large circular building that was almost never used as a dwelling, but instead as a place for social and ceremonial gatherings. Other, smaller structures were used for their dwellings. The assembly house was especially used for dancing.

Constructing a traditional assembly house was a community affair — everyone pitched in to help. For several months before actual building began, several men would gather the necessary timbers by burning down oak trees. With everyone working, construction took only four or five days. First they used digging sticks to excavate a large circular pit 3 or 4 feet deep and some 40 to 50 feet across. To determine the proper radius, four men would lie stretched out, with the feet of one touching the head of another. Next, the builders sank four large posts at the corners of a square in the center of the pit. The sides of the square were about as long as a man could reach by stretching both arms. They were connected at the top by horizontal poles.

Outside this central square, the Miwok sank eight smaller posts and rested additional poles on them, forming an octagon. They then rested a series of long willow roof beams around these supporting structures to form a flattened cone-like structure with a smoke hole at the center. Horizontal sticks lashed to these sloping poles supported a thatch of brush topped with long pine needles. Finally, the builders added a thick covering of earth to seal the entire structure from rain and winds. When finished, the roof would be 1½ to 2 feet thick.

At the ceremony that celebrated completion of the assembly house, the builders used their digging sticks to excavate a fire pit about 2 or 3 feet across and a foot deep. The fire pit was in the center of the structure, directly beneath the central smoke hole. Dances took place within the central square of timbers around the fire pit. Spectators watched from outside this central area.

When sawed lumber was introduced to Indian culture late in the nineteenth century, many central California groups began to build the roofs and walls of their roundhouses from planks, rather than packed earth. These newer assembly houses, which were built by the Maidu, Nomlaki, Pomo, and Wintu Indians, as well as the Miwok, had shingled roofs.

Today, a few vestiges of the roundhouse tradition still exist in Central California. For example, the Nomlaki Indians, who still live in Glenn County, west of the city of Chico, use a roundhouse for their ceremonies. Half earthlodge, half plank construction, it may well be the oldest California roundhouse still in use.

Nearly all Native American groups had a story of the theft of fire that took place when the world was new. For the Miwok, the assembly house played an important part in this story. It probably had a special meaning for the Miwok because the stories themselves were told in the assembly house at night when the central fire shone bright in the darkened house. Storytellers would travel from village to village, stopping in each to recite their stories. Villagers paid them with food and furs, baskets and beads. Storytelling might take all night, and included songs from the various characters in the story.

The animals of the creation stories lived on the earth before the creation of people and were thought of as nearly human. Each one had a special part to play. In this story, Coyote's interference causes the creation of different languages.

Long ago, all the world was dark. The mountain people decided they needed fire. Without it, they had to eat their meals cold and go around in the dark. They had nothing with which to heat their roundhouses. They talked among themselves a long time about how to get fire. Yet they came up with no good ideas.

Lizard, who was as lazy then as he is now, was lying on a rock looking into the valley. One especially lazy day as Lizard lay on his belly he saw something in the valley. He told Coyote, "I see flames down there in the valley. The Valley People have fire. We need someone to get it for us."

"Loo'looe, the White-footed Mouse is the best one to steal fire from the Valley People," said Coyote. "He is very swift and he plays the flute. We'd better send him."

They found Loo'looe in the roundhouse, playing his flute. "All right," said the little creature, "I'll do it."

Loo'looe set off on his quest, taking nothing but his flute. When he reached the valley, he began to play for the people he found there. They liked his flute playing so much that they arranged to give a big feast. They asked him to play for them in their roundhouse where everyone could hear his music.

When everyone had entered the roundhouse and was properly seated, Eagle took a big blanket made of condor feathers and used it to seal the door. Eagle did not trust Loo'looe and worried that he might attempt to steal something. The only opening left was the smoke hole in the roof.

Loo'looe sat down near the fire, with all the others sitting around him. As soon as he saw that he had everyone's attention, he began to play. His music was very beautiful and soothing. It made everyone feel happy. Loo'looe played on. After a time the people in the roundhouse began to yawn. So sweet was Loo'looe's music that they were soon fast asleep. Even Eagle, who had suspected the intentions of the white-footed mouse, fell asleep. Loo'looe kept on playing. He wanted to be sure that everyone was sleeping deeply.

When he finished his last melody, he rose quietly, tiptoed a few steps to the fire, and picked up all that was left — two small coals. Putting the coals in his flute, he stepped softly past his sleeping hosts. People were sprawled everywhere within the inner square of posts, so he had to be very careful where he stepped. Soon he was at the doorway. You can imagine his surprise to find that the doorway was blocked by the feather blanket Eagle had laid across it.

Loo'looe glanced back to see whether anyone had awakened and then set to work on the feather blanket. With his teeth he was soon able to cut through. Loo'looe ran out into the cold night and headed for the mountains.

Later, as it grew colder in the roundhouse, the people woke up to discover that the fire was gone and Loo'looe had disappeared. He must be the culprit, they thought, but who was fast enough to catch up with him? They sent Hail and Rain Shower, the only ones swift enough, after the little white-footed mouse.

Loo'looe saw them off in the distance, and ran even harder toward his own village's roundhouse. When he saw that they would overtake him before he reached it, he stopped next to a buckeye tree and placed one of the coals in it. The other he threw in a nearby stream. When Hail and Rain Shower caught up with him, the coals were nowhere to be seen. Though the two looked and looked, they were unable to find them.

After they left, Loo'looe reached into a hole in the buckeye tree and pulled the one coal out. It was still hot. Putting it into his flute again, Loo'looe took it to his people. The people put the coal into the pit in the center of the roundhouse and used it to light the firewood they had brought in. For the first time they could see inside the roundhouse, and they could cook their meat.

Coyote nearly destroyed Loo'looe's efforts when he brought in deer meat and put it right on top of the fire, almost putting it out. Because of Coyote, the roundhouse began to be cold again. Only the people near the fire could speak without their teeth chattering. The others, who were outside the central poles, grew so cold they could not speak clearly. Eventually the people divided into five groups. There were four groups on the outside — south, west, north, and east — each of which came to speak a different language. The middle group was different yet. Thus it happened that selfish Coyote drove the people apart. Today, people call him the greedy one because of his selfishness in taking all the fire for himself.

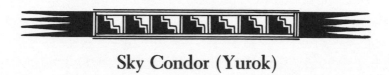

Sky Condor (Yurok)

In some respects, the Yurok Indians of Northern California bear greater similarity to the tribes of the Pacific Northwest than to their neighbors to the south. They lived among the forested hills and valleys on the lower Klamath River in the northwest corner of California. Like their northern neighbors, they built plank houses, and took a great interest in making fine tools and wooden household implements. In California, only the Chumash, many miles to the south, took as much interest in fashioning wooden objects.

The Yurok had an overwhelming interest in property and money. Everything, including marriages, births, and deaths, had its price, which could be paid for with finely worked dentalium shells, the Yurok's most important medium of exchange. Dentalium shells come in six varieties, each of different length. The Yurok obtained them as trade goods from other tribes, who took them from the Pacific Ocean and kept them on strings nearly 30 inches long. The importance of the dentalium shell to the Yurok is signified by the fact that they frequently refer to dentalium in their myths as if it were a man. In some myths, dentalium appears as a creator.

Next in importance to dentalium shells were woodpecker scalps. The Yurok prized two kinds, both of which were bright scarlet, and worked them into magnificent dance headdresses.

They also used them to trim other articles of display. In the following story, Sky Condor owned a beautiful, magic stick adorned with a woodpecker crest, which two brothers conspired to steal because it was so valuable. They buried it in their sweathouse, a structure of great importance to the Yurok.

The sweathouse was not always used for sweating. Men and grown boys worked, meditated, and visited with friends there. They also slept in the sweathouse, rather than with their families. Each Yurok sweathouse generally held six or seven men, who had regular places there in which to sleep.

Yurok sweathouses were shaped like an A-frame. They were smaller than houses, and the entire interior was dug into the earth about four feet. Planks at both ends supported a single ridgepole from which the roof planks were supported. The bottom end of the roof rested right on the earth, eliminating the need for side walls. The roof planks were highly uneven, which gave the building a rustic, unkempt look on the outside.

The interior, however, was always kept neat and clean. The floor was paved with neatly fitted stone slabs, or with smooth planks. A few feet from the middle was the fireplace, a hole about eighteen inches square and lined with flat stones.

The door, which was placed in the middle of one of the long sides, always faced the river or ocean. It was only about eighteen inches wide and a foot high. A second, smaller door, which served only as an exit, was carved in the center plank of one end. It could be closed by inserting a wooden plug carved to fit it. The exit door was used during ceremonial sweats, such as those in the morning and evening. Although the door was extremely small, the men could easily slip out after working up a good sweat.

The gathering of sweathouse firewood was an important function, one that was often mentioned in the myths. The proper way to gather firewood was to climb a tall fir tree and cut branches from near the top. When they held a sweat, the men would cut the branches into small lengths and burn them in the fire pit. The doors were plugged tight. Because the fire produced a lot of smoke, the sweater had to lie low on the ground to escape breathing too much smoke.

In the following myth, dentalium money, woodpecker scalps, and the sweathouse all play important roles. Each of these elements was extremely important in Yurok life. Although the boys found they could not kill Sky Condor in the sweathouse and keep his powerful and beautiful woodpecker-crest stick, by beating him in a battle of wits, they *were* able to gain treasure nevertheless.

Many years ago, two brothers embarked on an ocean fishing trip. The younger one would not look his older brother in the eye — he had something on his mind.

"What is wrong, little brother?" asked the older boy.

"There is nothing wrong," he replied, "you are just imagining things."

Their fishing trip continued in strained silence. The younger boy would not talk. The older one knew he would hear the same noncommital answer to any further questions so he was silent also.

When they returned and began to start a purifying fire in the sweathouse, the younger brother broke his long silence. "I have been thinking how to gain great power and treasure. I have been thinking about Sky Condor's magic woodpecker-crest stick. It is not only beautiful but very powerful. I want you to pretend to be dead. After he thinks you have been dead for a day or so, Sky Condor will come down from the sky and try to eat you. Then we can capture his woodpecker-crest stick. Will you try it?"

The older brother was surprised at the boldness of his younger brother's scheme, and not a little worried that it might fail and he really would be dead. Yet in the end he agreed.

The next day, the older brother prentended to die. Yet the younger brother did not bury him. He grieved loudly over his brother's faked death and decided to take him south along the coast to find a proper place to bury him. As he rowed in their canoe, he finally came to a place where there were two huge rocks just offshore.

"This is a good place," he said aloud. "I will bury him here."

Right there, the younger brother dug a large eagle-catching pit and laid his older brother in it. The next morning, he saw birds flying round the pit, some with woodpecker crests. Younger brother chased them off and waited.

The next morning, as he had expected, the younger brother saw Sky Condor flying toward them, hoping to eat the dead brother. He hid in the bushes and waited. Oh how beautiful was Sky Condor's woodpecker-crest stick!

When Sky Condor had descended into the pit, he lifted his stick to pierce the older brother. Just as he was about to strike, the younger one grabbed the stick away with a shout of joy.

"We have the magic stick, Brother, we have it. Awaken and follow me quickly." The two ran home with the woodpecker-crest stick that belonged to Sky Condor.

Sky Condor, who had been thoroughly tricked, was angry. But he was extremely fond of his woodpecker-crest stick so he flew up high and followed them at a distance. Soon the brothers arrived at their camp. They slipped through the front door of their sweathouse and buried the stick in the floor under one of the planks.

Sky Condor landed on top of the sweathouse and waited until the brothers came out. Then he entered and perched on top of the place where his stick was buried. He waited. "I won't move until you give me back my woodpecker-crest stick," warned Sky Condor.

The brothers built a great fire in the sweathouse, hoping that the giant bird would die from the heat. Each day, for ten days, they tried a different kind of wood in their fire. Each day the fire grew hotter. But supernatural beings like Sky Condor do not die easily, and all their efforts were in vain. Sky Condor simply waited on top of the mound, patiently, silently.

On the tenth day, Sky Condor spoke. "You see that you cannot kill me with heat. I want my stick back. Let me have it and I will reward you richly." By now the brothers had given up hope of killing him, and they agreed to give back the magic stick.

"Let me take you on a journey to a magic land," Sky Condor said to the younger brother. The brother agreed and he climbed on Sky Condor's back and they set off.

Sky Condor instructed the brother to close his eyes and not open them again, no matter what happened, until he was told it was safe. Oh, the things he heard and felt! Great was his temptation to look around and see what was happening. Yet the brother did as he was told, and kept his eyes tightly closed.

Finally they arrived at a place where there was a beach full of money (dentalium shells). Everywhere, money was washed up on shore. The younger brother was extremely excited and wanted to take as much as he could back with him. Sky Condor told him that he could take only one piece of money. He showed him one that was welded together with another piece. "Take only this one," he said sternly.

With this they flew back to the camp where the older brother waited in the sweathouse.

"Put the money in a small basket and keep it covered for five days," Sky Condor told the brothers. "After five days, look in the basket. Then put the money you find in a larger basket and then a larger one every five days until you have enough to live on comfortably for the rest of your days." The brothers nodded agreement.

"When you have enough, do not change baskets any longer. I am going up into the sky now. Come and see me sometime."

"No, I can't follow you where you are going," replied the younger brother.

"Very well, but be sure to follow my instructions about the money or you won't have anything."

"We will. Thank you." Younger Brother was sad to see Sky Condor going. He had grown quite fond of him.

Sky Condor flew off to the south. The brothers, whose cleverness had fooled Sky Condor, were now quite rich.

In the Beginning (Yurok)

Yurok houses were highly unusual. The Yurok used no posts or beams in their houses but built them entirely of planks split from redwood logs. Using elkhorn wedges and large stone mauls, they split the planks and sometimes smoothed the surface of the roughest ones with an adze. Each end of the Yurok house was made of thick vertical planks up to ten feet long or more, sunk a few feet in the earth. The boards, which might be from one to four feet wide, were held in place with two horizontal poles, one on the inside, one outside, which were lashed together with grapevines passed through holes in the boards. The side walls were only a few feet high and were also made of planks sunk in the ground.

As the following story notes, the houses of well-to-do families had roofs with two peaks; the smaller houses owned by poorer families had only one peak. In a Yurok house, the roof planks were supported by poles that ran the length of the building between the vertical end planks. Two thicknesses of thin roof boards were simply laid across these poles. A two-peaked house had three roof pitches. The ends of the roof planks overhung the sides of the house to make long eaves. Most Euro-American visitors to Yurok villages thought these houses looked rather untidy, as the roof planks were of all different lengths and the lower ends were not squared off.

A smoke hole was made by propping up one of the roof planks, or pushing it aside in dry weather. The family entered and left their house by slipping though a round hole about two feet across in one of the largest, thickest planks in the end wall. The bottom of the doorway was a few inches above the ground. The door was a plank that slid open and closed. Houses faced so the door opened toward the downstream direction. The Yurok oriented their entire world to whichever river or creek they lived along.

The house interior was particularly unusual. Persons entering had to pass through a narrow storage area just inside the circular door. The rest of the house was on two levels. In the center was a pit from two to five feet deep, the sides of which were carefully lined with smooth, thin slabs of wood. When

indoors, the family spent its time in the lower level, living and working around a central fire. The upper area, which was on a level with the earth outside, was used primarily for storage. Large storage baskets, utensils, tools, and food generally covered this space. The women and children slept in the house. The men slept in the sweathouse.

The following story takes place in the Beginning Time when the world was not quite finished. In the boy's dream, he meets Wetskak, the name of the smallest dentalium, one of six kinds of these shells that the Yurok and other California tribes used as money. Wetskak was sometimes referred to as "young man's money" because it was so small. In this case, Wetskak shows the boy how to build a house.

Once a boy lived all alone at the edge of the world. But he did not live well. He was lonely and wanted someone to talk to. He wanted to know about the world. Before he started off to see the world, he decided to sleep in his sweathouse. "Maybe I'll dream about the world," he thought.

In his dream, he heard a noise outside and thought, "I'm sure that is someone to talk to."

The person entered the boy's sweathouse. "I am sorry that you live alone like this. It is good that you have a sweathouse, but you shall have other things as well. Come outside with me," said the stranger. "I will show you."

"First I will help you build a house."

"What is a house?" asked the boy.

"It is a place to live."

The person showed him how to build a house. The two gathered and split several long planks and set them in the earth to make the ends of the house. Then they built the long sides by setting shorter planks in the earth. Finally, they lifted a pole in place between the two ends and laid roof planks down. This house had just one ridgepole.

"I don't think it looks quite right," said the boy.

"Yes, we will build a bigger house."

This time the two built a house that had two ridgepoles. The person said, "I have traveled all over the world and seen other houses. As long as the world exists, houses will be like these two. Poor families will have houses with only one ridgepole. Rich ones will have the larger ones. We will make it so."

"Who are you?" asked the boy. "Where do you come from? I thought I was the only person living in the world. I have grown up by myself."

The person smiled and said, "Do not think that you could have grown if I had not made it possible. I grew first. I know all about the world as it is now. But it is incomplete. I will make the world as it will be in the future. I will finish the world."

"Yes, but who are you?" asked the boy.

"Many there are in the world who would like to know who I am. But I will tell you later what I will become, after this world is complete."

"Please tell me now," said the boy, impatient to know who his newfound friend was.

"Well, I can tell you now. But do not tell anyone else, even if they should ask. Later, when I have finished the world, I shall become what the humans call dentalium."

"Really? What will your name be?"

"There are six kinds of dentalia. I shall be one of them, the smallest, but a pretty one. People will call me Wetskak.

"But that will happen later. First, I must finish the world. We will start in the morning."

The boy was pleased that he would finally get to see the world, and kept on dreaming.

6 Painted Planks and Totem Poles
Northwest Coast Dwellings

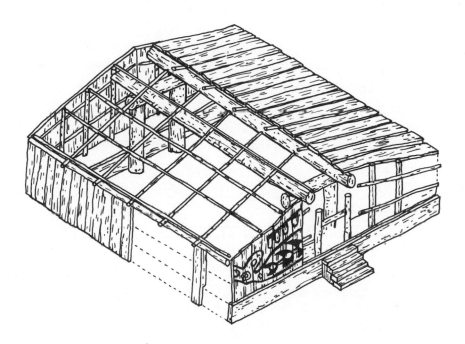

The craggy shores, sheltered bays, and thick forests of the Northwest Coast from Alaska to Oregon provided a fruitful life for the dozens of tribes that lived there. Before European diseases took their toll and white settlers displaced them from the land, tribal groups lived well off abundant coastal sea life — salmon, herring, smelt, shellfish, and even whale. These foods were supplemented by animals, birds, berries, and seeds from the inland valleys.

Northwest Coast summers are relatively cool, and the winter seldom brings freezing temperatures. The moderate climate and varied food sources allowed these tribes much free time to develop a complex society and sophisticated arts. These Indians became the premier woodworkers of the Americas. Using only tools of stone and bone, they excelled in building large wooden houses, with plank walls and roofs. Some of their dwellings were decorated with wonderfully carved house-poles and painted fronts.

Northwest Coast woodworkers used all of the local woods in their crafts, but preferred red cedar for its softness and even grain, which made it easy to work. Red cedar was particularly useful for making house roofs and siding because it is relatively light and could be split easily into long, straight planks by using the stone tools that were available. Red cedar was so important to the woodworkers' home economy that they believed the tree had great spiritual power. They shredded its inner bark and used the strands to weave fine baskets, hats, mats, rope, and even cloth. The outer bark they often used to roof their houses.

When the first European travelers explored this part of North America in the eighteenth century, they discovered immediately that the region would provide an abundant source of food and other natural resources such as lumber and skins. They were amazed to discover how well the native peoples, who gathered foods and hunted for a living, were able to turn their environment to their own advantage. The Europeans found tribes with many different languages and customs who had developed the ability to fashion highly effective fish traps, nets, and harpoons, and to build graceful, seaworthy canoes. They also wove fine baskets, mats, and clothes from a variety of natural materials.

From late fall through the winter, most groups lived in well-constructed plank houses located in sheltered bays or along inland streams. Tribes were divided into several different clans, each with its own ancestral animal or bird. Each clan house, built according to plans handed down by the ancestors of their myths, served as home to several families. Each family had its own space where it prepared food over its own fire, slept, and worked at indoor chores.

The interiors of the houses seemed cluttered to European eyes. Drying fish hung from the ceiling or from poles; wooden storage boxes, baskets, and cooking utensils were stored haphazardly on overhead scaffolds; and gathering baskets often littered the floor. Some tribes decorated their house interiors with carved house posts, or with elaborately carved and painted screens. These decorations illustrated scenes from their myths.

In late spring, many groups would move to less sheltered areas along the coast, taking most of their households with them. They would remove the planks from the supporting framework, tie them between canoes, and move an entire household — goods, house, family, and all — to their summer encampment. Because the long days of summer allowed the Northwest Coast tribes to spend much more time out of doors, their summer homes were generally less elaborate than their winter dwellings. More temporary campsites, used for hunting, gathering, or fishing, might be quite basic and consist of slabs of bark or mats laid over a simple framework of sticks.

Each tribe had its own style of house. For example, in the southern region, near where Seattle is now, eighteenth-century explorer George Vancouver came across a Coast Salish house that was home to over six hundred individuals. The Salish called it *Tsu-Suc-Cub*, or Old-Man-House. This enormous dwelling had a simple shed-type roof typical of the Puget Sound region and stretched nearly a fifth of a mile along the coast. The posts supporting the front of Old-Man-House stood about 20 feet high. Much longer roof poles sloped from these posts down to rear support posts that were 5 or 6 feet high. Roof planks on Salish shed-type houses were not fastened down, but were deliberately left free so they could be moved to let smoke out. The Salish used large rocks to secure the planks against the occasional high winds.

The Tlingit, the Tsimshian, and the Haida, who live to the north in and near Alaska, brought house building and carved house poles to a fine art. Both the Tlingit and the Tsimshian were well known for painting the fronts of their houses. These were not just decorations, but clan symbols representing the story of the clan's origins.

Blue Jay's House

Although the Quinault Indians on the coast southwest of Mount Olympus in Washington speak a dialect of the Salish language and follow traditional customs similar to those of their tribal cousins of Puget Sound, their traditional houses had gabled roofs instead of the shed style more common to their Salish neighbors. Houses varied in length from thirty to sixty feet and might be twenty to forty feet wide. In villages, the houses were all oriented east–west and were arranged in rows along the river bank. Two to four families, each with its own fire and personal area, might occupy a house.

In building their houses, the Quinault laid the roof planks horizontally along the length of the house. They would start at the bottom of the roof along the eaves and work upward, leaving each upper plank to overlap the one below it so the roof would shed water and keep out strong winds. Unlike the roof planks of shed construction, which were loosely laid and held down only with large stones, Quinault roof planks were firmly lashed. The two planks meeting at the gable overlapped and were fastened only at their lower edges. Thus, individuals inside the house could push roof planks open from the inside to allow light to enter and smoke to escape. The Quinault chinked cracks between vertical wall planks with moss or fastened narrow planks across the gaps.

Quinault houses had a plank platform in the front that was used as a work area. Also, on sunny days, the old men of the village would gather there, sitting against the house on plank benches, to take in the sun and to gossip. They might sit there just to "watch the earth," as the Quinault say.

The knowledge of how to build a sturdy, warm, dry house was an essential part of adult life. In the following tale, Blue Jay, who is always a clown in Coast Salish stories, shows us the behavior characteristic of this bragging bird by building the roof of his house backward, from the peak to the eave. As a result, it leaked profusely.

One day, Blue Jay decided to build a house for himself. He had carefully watched other people build their houses, and was sure he knew how. First, he gathered all the posts and planks he would need. Then he dug holes into the ground and set upright posts deep in the ground so they would support the walls and roof — four along one side, and four along the other. At the ends between the rows he planted two posts to hold the roof peak. Finally, he carefully lashed rafters to the posts to provide support for the roof. So far, so good, he thought.

Stepping back from this framework, he walked proudly around his new house, gazing at his handiwork. Blue Jay was very pleased with himself and set about putting up the walls. He selected planks long enough to stretch all the way from the eaves into the ground. Blue Jay knew that the wall boards of snug houses must be set firmly into the ground.

After he had rested a bit, Blue Jay stepped importantly around his new house once more and started to build the roof. Yet, instead of starting at the eave, he climbed right up to the peak, huffing and puffing because the boards were very heavy. Taking the first plank, he placed it against the peak of the roof. The next plank he arranged so it overlapped the first. Working downward, he made every plank overlap the one above it, tying it down to the rafter below in good Quinault fashion. Then he repeated the process for the other side. My, he was proud of himself!

Finally, he built a platform in front and a plank bench so he could sit outside and enjoy the sunset. He was so pleased with his handiwork that he moved in right away.

No sooner had he settled in his house and sat down on his plank bench to enjoy the fruits of his labor than a violent rainstorm began to move along the river toward him. Confident that he would be snug in his house, he moved just inside the doorway to watch the storm approach. "My, how the wind is blowing," he said to no one in particular. "But *I'll* be safe and dry in *my* house."

When the rain hit, he felt some rain drops, so he moved farther in, away from the door. To his dismay, the rain only fell harder. Looking up, he saw the rain pouring through the long cracks in his roof. He had built his roof so the rain poured down each plank and under the next one below it.

"Oh, what do those people know about building a house?" he said aloud. "They must have shown me the wrong way. I'll fix those leaks." Then he grabbed his bow and shot arrows at every place he saw a leak.

He shot arrow after arrow. For all I know Blue Jay may still be there trying to fix those leaks.

Thunderbird Helps Salmon Build a House

Entering a painted Kwakiutl house on Vancouver Island was like walking into the mouth of an enormous monster. Indeed, the Kwakiutl thought of the house as a living being, belonging to the entire family line, not to any particular occupant. The paintings on the front of these houses, and their carved houseposts, carried images symbolizing the families' ancestors. Each house had a name.

Stories from the dawn of time explain how the Kwakiutl people learned to build houses. In those days, people moved back and forth between the realms of animals and fish and humans as easily as we might change clothes today. In this

story, the creator, in the form of Thunderbird, helps the first
man in the land of the Nimkish, one of the tribes of the
Kwakiutl nation, build his house.

Once, in the days before the great flood, Salmon swam up a large river. After
a long time, he tired and decided to go ashore to rest. When he climbed onto
dry land, Salmon became a man.

When the waters of the great flood crept over the face of the land, Salmon
wisely decided to return to his former fish shape until the water subsided. A long
time passed, but finally a day came when the water began to pull back from the
tops of the mountains.

The sea steadily retreated and dry land once again became visible. Salmon
saw this and decided to go ashore and turn into a man again. Since he had no
shelter, Salmon began to build a house for himself.

Salmon's only tool was a stone adze that he used to shape and finish the logs.
With his adze, he shaped posts for the walls. Then he dug a hole for each post
and set the posts firmly in place. As he carefully shaped the beams for the roof
of his house, he realized he had a serious problem: the roof beams were very
heavy and he had no one to help him lift them into place. As Salmon sat on a
rock, pondering his problem, he heard a sudden noise nearby. It sounded like
a great rushing of wind with a low rumble like thunder.

Salmon looked around and saw a huge bird settling itself on a boulder.
Salmon recognized the bird as a supernatural being, and said, "Oh, great
Thunderbird, I am indeed a very lucky man. Until I saw you I felt very sad
because I could not finish building my house. I have been granted a great
vision."

Thunderbird replied, "I can help you. Indeed, that is why I am here." With
this, he removed his Thunderbird mask.

Then Thunderbird grasped one of the roof beams in his powerful talons,
flew up over the walls of the house, and put the beam lightly in place. He
repeated this until all four roof beams were secure atop the house posts.
When Thunderbird finished, he returned to his boulder and took off his cov-

ering of feathers and wings, becoming a man and helped Salmon finish the house.

Thunderbird said to Salmon, "In the future, make a thunderbird mask and a cape of feathers and huge wings. Become Thunderbird. When danger threatens your people, make a great thunder by flapping your wings. Make thunder when a man dies, too. Flash your eyes to make the lightning. Fold your wings and stand tall to symbolize peace for your people."

The place was named Thunderbird Place and still bears this name today.

The House of Myths

The Bella Coola of British Columbia, who live northeast of the Kwakiutl, tell of a wonderful house in the sky where all their ancestor myths are stored. They call it Nusmata, The House of Myths. The gods Senx, the sun, and the creator, Alkuntam, live there. This sky lodge of Alkuntam became the model for the Bella Coola's own earthly houses. Bella Coola storytellers often recount the story of The House of Myths at their ceremonial gatherings.

In the beginning time Alkuntam lived with Senx in Nusmata. Their house was large and contained all manner of wonderful beings, for it was The House of Myths, which held the cloaks of all the ancestors. From the highest point of Nusmata, way up at the peak, the face of a grizzly bear stared down. In front stood a post that was painted with many different kinds of birds. White crane perched atop the post.

Senx and Alkuntam lived in a room at the back of the house. It was dangerous to visit them because near their room lived the cannibal monster, Baexolla. Whenever the two gods wanted to destroy someone, they would lead him near the room of Baexolla, who would rush out and devour the hapless victim.

Senx was busy half the day lighting up the world, so he had little time for Alkuntam, who became desperately lonely. One day Alkuntam decided to create four carpenter-gods to help him, one for each of the four directions. The carpenters gave humans the arts of building, carving, and painting. But first the carpenters made worker-gods to help them. These workers set about to carve all the Bella Coola ancestors out of sacred cedar. After they painted the ancestors, they made the moon, the stars, and all the animals, birds, trees, and flowers.

After the workers had completed their tasks, Alkuntam invited each of the ancestors to wear one of the bird or animal cloaks that hung on the walls of The House of Myths. Wrapped in their cloaks, each ancestor then turned into the bird or animal of the cloak. Alkuntam gave them names and sent them to earth, where they gave up their cloaks and took on human form. Their cloaks floated to the sky to take their places again on the walls of Nusmata.

The Grizzly-Bear House

One of the most important ceremonials the Northwest Coast Indians had in common was called the "potlatch," a Chinook Indian term that means giving a gift. The potlatch was an elaborate formal party hosted by a tribal chief and his house group for another chief or chiefs and their families. What distinguished the potlatch from other large feasts, which the Northwest Coast Indians also held, was the practice of giving gifts to the guests. A potlatch was held to provide the appropriate setting for making an important announcement, such as the marriage of a son or daughter, or the birth of an heir who would eventually inherit a prestigious title, a crest, or certain tribal privileges. The potlatch served to validate the announcement, much as witnesses at a wedding support and validate the marriage.

In the case of the transfer of title or privilege, a potlatch had the additional purpose of giving tribal recognition to the transfer. Even though an individual might be the only possible heir to a title, he had no automatic right to it or to the privileges that accompanied the title, until a potlatch was held. One of the common privileges, for example, was the right to fish in a particular stream. The individual could not exercise that right or allow others to use it until the potlatch announcing the transfer of power occurred. During the potlatch the group's legendary history would be recited — how the title or privilege had been acquired by an ancestor, who in the family had possessed it, and how it was transmitted. After a feast, and the recitation, gifts in the name of the person for whom the potlatch was held would be passed out to the assembled guests.

This story relates the founding of the ancient village of Nusqalst, on the shores of one of the many rivers flowing into the Bella Coola in Canadian British Columbia.

At the beginning of time, a man named Kamalsonx came down to earth from the sky. Alkuntam, the creator, sent with him a present to the village of Nusqalst from his house — a model of Nusmata, The House of Myths, for Kamalsonx to live in.

Kamalsonx remembered well his stay in Nusmata before he came to earth. On the roof peak, he had seen the face of a huge grizzly bear. Kamalsonx used this grizzly bear symbol on everything he owned. He used it on blankets, storage boxes, tools, utensils, and to decorate the interior of his house.

Kamalsonx's unusual house lasted for many generations. He made the door in the shape of a grizzly bear's mouth that would open to admit visitors and close once they were inside. Whenever Kamalsonx gave a ceremonial potlatch, the house would magically grow to accommodate whatever number of guests entered. Before the grizzly-bear-mouth door, a huge fat man named Booksta lay on his back. Anyone entering had to step first on Booksta's fat stomach, then through the grizzly bear mouth. When an ordinary person, a slave, or commoner stepped on Booksta, he was quiet. When a chief, or other man of high rank stepped on his stomach, he would grunt loudly. His noisy response would announce the arrival of someone special, a weighty person, we might say. The louder his "ouff," the more important the person.

Kamalsonx loved to give potlatches and began to prepare early in the spring for his winter potlatch. There was much work to be done and many hunting trips were necessary to be sure he had enough food for the festivities. Because he invited many people from many different tribes, Kamalsonx had to build extra shelters for them to sleep in. For each potlatch, Kamalsonx painted the back wall of his house with pictures of the sun, moon, special stars, and constellations, as well as pictures showing great deeds of bravery.

For the potlatch, Kamalsonx wore a huge grizzly bear skin — carrying its enormous head above his own. When all his guests were ready, he began to dance. As Kamalsonx danced, a large box quietly appeared from a secret hole in the floor. It was decorated with a large raven, a symbol of great power. The box held a number of gifts for one visiting tribe — exactly the right number of gifts! Then the raven box would disappear and the dancing would continue. Soon the box would reappear with exactly the right number of gifts for another guest tribe. The ritual continued until he had honored all guest tribes and groups. This special feature of the potlatch was one of the things Kamalsonx had seen when he visited Nusmata. Alkuntam ordered gift-giving at future potlatches to be done this same way.

These first Nusqalst people erected special portrayals of their sacred five-peaked mountain, which they put in front of their potlatch house. On one peak there was always the figure of a mountain goat, which had been brought to earth in the beginning by the ancestors to be their staple food.

Keethit, the Killer-Whale House

The Tlingits especially value the killer whale, because it is strong, brave, and capable of killing whales, which the Tlingits hunted for food and blubber off the coast of Alaska. The southern Alaska Killer-Whale House people claim a man named Natsihlanae, who made the first killer whales, as their ancestor. One of their houses, Keethit, is their ancestral house.

The Killer-Whale people painted the front of another of their clan houses, called the "Killer-Whale Dorsal Fin House," with large images of two whales, set tail to tail. On the inside wall, Tlingit artisans carved a killer whale chasing a seal.

The story of Natsihlanae is both a moral tale and one that illustrates the close ties that the Tlingit and other Northwest Coast tribes felt with the fish and mammals they hunted for food and clothing. The story recognizes implicitly that sea lions understand the need of humans to hunt sea lions for food, just as sea lions hunt fish to survive. When they act correctly, the hunter and the hunted both help to maintain the proper balance of nature.

Natsihlanae's brothers-in-law once upset this balance by attempting to abandon him. In rescuing Natsihlanae, the chief of the sea lions helps him avenge the wrong done to him. The ancestor of the Killer-Whale House people restores the proper balance by carving eight killer whales to help him hunt and to punish his brothers-in-law.

An old man, Natsihlanae, was a great and successful hunter. His brothers-in-law in his wife's village were very envious of his skill. One day the village men went out to hunt sea lions.

As they neared shore, Natsihlanae jumped from the canoe and began to spear many sea lions. The brothers-in-law enviously watched him work. How easily he made kill after kill! So they sneaked back to their canoe and left him there alone. Natsihlanae was working so hard that he didn't even see or hear the canoe leaving until it was well out in deep water. Though Gaxa, the youngest of the brothers-in-law, tried to make them stay, the others refused to listen to him. "We will fix our brother-in-law so he can't hunt anymore."

"Where are you going?" Natsihlanae shouted to his brothers-in-law, who were paddling away from the island. "Come back." But they ignored him and were soon out of sight.

Natsihlanae continued to spear sea lions until he was too tired to continue. He lay down to sleep. Before long, a raucous shrieking awakened him. It was Sea Gull, who took pity on him and came to help.

Sea Gull led Natsihlanae to the house of the chief of the Sea-Lion people, who told the mighty hunter that his son had been wounded by Natsihlanae's spear. The hunter was so grateful for the hospitality and so sorry for spearing the chief's son, that he healed the boy.

Then the chief said he would send Natsihlanae back to his people. He blew up a large sea lion skin and told Natsihlanae to climb in. The chief put the skin in the water and told Natsihlanae to think only of his home and he would soon be there. And so it happened.

When he got back to the village, Natsihlanae gathered his tools and began carving killer whales out of different kinds of wood. Each time, he sang a song to them and told them to swim. But his first three attempts simply floated on their sides.

Finally, he tried yellow cedar. After carving eight killer whales, he sang to them and told them to swim. This time his efforts were successful. The cedar killer whales swam out and brought him food. Then Natsihlanae told the eight whales to attack his brothers-in-law's canoe and to save only his friend Gaxa. When they brought Gaxa to him, Natsihlanae told the killer whales to go back out to sea and to help humans from then on and never to harm them. To this day, whale fat crackles in the fire just like yellow cedar.

On the spot where Natsihlanae carved the killer whales, the Daqtlawedi Clan built a Killer-Whale House. On the crest of the house they carved a large whale. The house was situated so that when the west wind blew through special openings in the wall, it made a mournful sound.

This sad wailing sound inspired a song about a man who left his home and went to a strange land among strange people. This song is always used at the feasts of the Killer-Whale people. The melancholy theme of the whale song is a universal symbol of homesickness to this day.

The Sea-Raven House

The Tsimshian were especially noted for building houses made of smooth planks, finely adzed, and carefully fitted together. Their homes, which might be thirty feet on a side, were generally built with gabled roofs, supported by two large beams set about halfway between the gable and the outside wall. Walls were made of wide planks set horizontally in grooves in the houseposts. The focal point of most daily activities was the fire pit, located at the center of the house under the smoke hole in the roof. It was surrounded by a larger sunken plank-lined area that accommodated the work and social activities of family members.

Like many another Northwest Coast group, the Tsimshian took great pride in their houses. Tsimshian chiefs competed with each other to have the most elaborate and beautiful house paintings and interior screens. Tsimshian craftsmen painted many of their house fronts with scenes illustrating an incident from their mythological past. Raven, Killer Whale, Bear, Eagle, Halibut, and even Sun, Moon, Stars, and Rainbow, could be seen on Tsimshian houses a century ago. In most cases the paintings represented stories of the clan's most important ancestor, who met with supernatural beings while fishing or hunting.

The Sea-Raven House tale, gathered from a storyteller belonging to the Ganhada clan, explains the origin of a house painted with the image of a monster known as Sea Raven. Sea Raven was one version of a monster called Snag of the Sand-

bar, who could be seen swimming and diving and grabbing everything that passed by it. Sea Raven acted just like a real sandbar snag — a log or large branch stuck in the sand, which snatches up everything the tide brings by. Early in the morning or near dusk, such snags must have seemed very much like monsters reaching out toward Tsimshian canoes carried to them by the currents.

Far in the past a young Ganhada hunter set out in his canoe early one autumn morning. He often hunted alone, sometimes for days at a time, and usually was one of the most successful hunters in his tribe. So when he pushed his canoe out into the cold early-morning water on this particular day, he was confident he would bring home many seals and sea otters.

For three days, however, the young man caught nothing! "Where are all the seals and sea otters that usually beg to be caught?" he wondered.

At nightfall, weary from his third long, unsuccessful day, the man hauled his canoe into the bushes by the shore, covered himself with his cloak, and slept. This night he dreamed that he would have great luck in the morning.

Before even the earliest sunlight had frightened away all the stars, he excitedly launched his canoe and set out for deep water. Morning Star was still hovering on the horizon when he saw a wondrous sight. A huge raven, Snag of the Sandbar, was flying toward him over the clear water, diving, hovering, and diving again. The monster bird repeated this many times. Fearful, yet deeply curious, the man crouched in the bottom of his canoe and watched carefully.

Snag of the Sandbar flapped his wings and flew directly over the little canoe. Looking up, the man could see many people under the wings of the monster bird. He breathed a sharp sigh of relief when the frightening creature of the air passed overhead, leaving him safe. This seemed like a powerful omen for his people.

When the young hunter returned home, he told the people what he had seen. Then he built a house and painted the front with the sea raven, Snag of the Sandbar.

Nagunaks, Chief of the Sea

The Tsimshian ancestors often met various supernatural beings while hunting, fishing, or traveling. This tale relates the story of a powerful Tsimshian chief named Dragging Along Shore who accidentally encountered Nagunaks while out hunting. In this story, Nagunaks appears as a whirlpool, enforcing the prohibition against hurting fish. In other versions he is a reef that causes canoes to crash. The Smithsonian Institution in Washington, D.C., owns a 38-foot housefront from Port Simpson that portrays the story of Nagunaks. It shows the Chief of the Sea in the center, surrounded above by the mermaids that always accompany him, with two killer whales on either side swimming toward him.

A very long time ago, Dragging Along Shore led a small hunting party of two Killer-Whale clansmen and his brother-in-law, an Eagle clansman. The four men left their village to hunt sea otters, sea lions, seals, and fish. They paddled along the coast for many days without catching anything at all.

"Let's go home," Dragging Along Shore told the others one evening just before dark. "We are having no luck out on the water. We will leave at first light." The others reluctantly agreed — hating to return to camp empty-handed.

The four men cast out their huge anchor-stone and settled down in their canoe for the night. Soon all were asleep. The men were unaware that, when they dropped their anchor-rock, it had fallen on the house of the sea-monster, Nagunaks. Nagunaks sent his slave girl, the beautiful blue cod, to the surface to see what the trouble was.

Dragging Along Shore was awakened by great splashings of the blue cod, swimming and playing beside the canoe. "You are keeping me awake!" he shouted at her. "Be quiet!" The cod kept splashing. The hunter had been away from home many days and needed his sleep for the long trip home. When she came close again, he swept her up out of the water and angrily broke her fins. Casting her back into the sea, he said, "She will bother me no more this night!"

The poor wounded fish returned to Chief Nagunaks' cave and told her story. "One of the hunters in the canoe broke my fins for splashing," she cried. The chief ordered his people to bring the canoe into his house at the bottom of the sea.

When the four tribesmen awoke, they discovered that they no longer lay at anchor in the inlet, but in a great and beautiful cave. "Can we all be having the same dream?" they wondered as they looked about in awe.

Mouse Woman came to Dragging Along Shore and asked, "Do you know who owns this cave?"

"No, I do not have any idea!"

"You are guests in the house of Chief Nagunaks," said Mouse Woman. "You hit the roof of his house with your anchor-stone, and he took you in. You treated Blue Cod badly, but if you show you have a good heart and treat the Sea people properly, you will be rewarded." She then advised him to offer the chief gifts and to do exactly as he was instructed.

In the meantime, Nagunaks had told his people to cook four seals — one for each guest.

"Open your mouth wide, Dragging Along Shore," instructed Nagunaks' slave. Remembering what Mouse Woman had said, he opened his mouth and swallowed the whole seal. Two other clansmen did the same.

However, the steersman, who was of the Eagle clan, was unable to swallow the seal whole. Chief Nagunaks gave orders that it be cut into portions for him to eat.

At the end of their visit, Nagunaks called for a great feast. He invited all the sea monsters that lived in underwater rock caves. There were a great many of them and they came from all parts of the world.

Dragging Along Shore realized that he should give the chief some gifts for taking them in, but they were on a hunting trip and had brought no gifts. Then he remembered that many of the ordinary items they carried for a hunting trip might be prized in this undersea kingdom.

"We have brought you presents," said Dragging Along Shore to Chief Nagunaks. "Let me see them," the chief replied. Dragging Along Shore and his men brought out coppers, goat fat, tobacco, crabapples, cranberries, and many other things and gave them to the Chief. Nagunaks was delighted with his gifts.

The feast was a wonderful one. All the sea monsters came. Some the men recognized as helpful monsters; but there were also all manner of other ones: some who were nasty and violent, and some who were just plain ugly. All vowed not to hurt human beings in the future. Dragging Along Shore pledged that his people would not hurt the animals of the sea. Many gifts were exchanged. Chief Nagunaks told all the monster chiefs of the wonderful gifts he had been given by Dragging Along Shore. Then Chief Nagunaks gave gifts to all the monsters and to Dragging Along Shore.

To Dragging Along Shore, he gave his own cloak and crest, his own copper canoe, copper stern-board and paddles, and a carved room. Chief Nagunaks' house was large. It had one large central room with a carved room on each side inside the house. One side room had two killer whales carved in it, nose to nose. The other side room, which held the copper canoe, paddles, and bailer, was carved with green seaweed.

Before the four left, the Chief took his hat and gave it to the steersman. He also gave him a large sea-apple with a living person inside and a box lined with abalone shell.

When the feast was over and the gifts given, Chief Nagunaks told the men to sleep aboard their new canoe.

The four hunters left for home the following morning in the copper canoe. It literally flew across the sea. Although their stay with the Chief seemed but a few days, when they reached home, they found they had been gone for a year.

The first of the tribe to see the men was Dragging Along Shore's oldest sister. She was out in the early morning light, mourning her brother whom she had last seen more than a year earlier. Yet what she saw at first was not a canoe with four men, but a huge monster that seemed to be alive, floating toward camp, making a loud bell-like noise. She was about to run from the shore when the monster turned into a canoe carrying the lost men. She alerted the camp and a great feast was given for the returned fishermen.

In time, Chief Dragging Along Shore went out fishing again with three clansmen. Although he had warned the tribe not to harm any fish, he forgot to remind those fishing with him of the taboos from Nagunaks. As usual, the hunters collected seal, otter, fish, and sea lions that just magically came up to the boat. Two of the hunters found a dead bullhead fish. They played with him and cut his mouth wide open before throwing him back into the sea.

When Nagunaks saw what had happened, he turned angry and created a huge whirlpool that drowned the two hunters and also brought his friend Dragging Along Shore into his cave to live with him. The remaining man who did not participate in the desecration returned to his people to remind them of the sea monster's taboo.

The clans used symbols of the gifts of Nagunaks to decorate their houses. From this time onward, they had more respect toward the sea and the sea animals and lived in peace with the sea monsters.

7 Painted Tipis

House Legends of the Plains

To ride into a Blackfoot Indian Sun Dance camp on the vast American Plains a hundred years ago was to enter into a world of open spaces, horses, strange sights, and strange smells. A Sun Dance camp consisted of hundreds of smoke-darkened tipis spread out across a grassy plain in a circle perhaps a mile around. From each tipi curled wisps of smoke, sending tantalizing smells of cooking food into the air.

Herds of horses grazed on the lush bunch-grass of nearby hills. Men and women in colorful clothes busied themselves in preparations for the sacred Sun Dance about to be held. Children playing the Blackfoot game of hoop and pole would chase after each other, dodging in and out of the enormous circle of tipis. Dogs followed closely behind, racing and tumbling with abandon across the open spaces. The movement and the cheerful sounds, smells, and bright colors spoke of ceremony and celebration.

Inside the larger circle was a smaller one of painted tipis. These tipis belonged to the head families of the various Blackfoot bands and were noticeably larger than the other lodges. Even from a distance, it would have been easy to see that each of them was painted with brightly colored images. Birds, animals, and serpents, sun, moon, and stars, even abstract designs, graced these special tipis.

The paintings on Blackfoot tipis were done for religious purposes, not for the sake of decoration. The painted tipi announced to the tribe that the family kept a sacred bundle and the rituals that went with it. The tipi design, the contents of the sacred bundle, and the rituals had been revealed to their owners in visions and dreams, and belonged only to them. Although their owners might pass the right to use the tipi design on to another, give him the sacred bundle, and teach him the rituals, no one was allowed simply to copy them.

Most Blackfoot painted tipis had black or dark blue tops, symbolizing the night sky. Clusters of white circles represented constellations like the Big Dipper and the Pleiades. The Blackfoot call the Big Dipper the Seven Stars, or Seven Brothers — seven brothers who climbed to the sky with their little sister to evade an evil older sister. They call the Pleiades the Bunched Stars — six poor brothers who rose to the sky to escape bad treatment from the other children in their band. Some tipis might also show cross-shaped symbols of Morning Star, the son of the sun.

The Blackfoot might also depict clouds, lightning, or the rainbow on their tipis, all powerful symbols of the sky. Certain animals or birds, as well, imparted special powers to the tipi. For example, deer and elk were strong helpers of the Blackfoot, as were eagle and raven. The most sacred animal was the beaver. Any of these animals might be depicted on a painted tipi, depending on the vision or dream that guided the tipi's designer. Around the bottom, the Blackfoot often painted a band of white circles, representing falling stars, which they revered as sacred messengers from the sky.

But the paintings of buffalo carried the greatest power, for it was the buffalo that provided food, clothing, tools, shelter, and even fuel for Plains dwellers like the Blackfoot. The Plains Indians ate every edible part of the buffalo, including the liver, intestines, and tongue. The skin furnished leather for clothing, tipi covers, bags and other containers, fur for weaving and rope, and sinew for thread. Buffalo bones were shaped and used for spoons, scrapers, and awls. Bladders provided jugs for carrying liquids. When wood was unavailable, they burned dried buffalo dung in their campfires.

The Snow Tipi

The Snow Tipi was owned by Chief Mad Wolf. His story of the Snow Tipi, told over a hundred years ago, illustrates the importance of the buffalo to the Blackfoot. When Sacred Otter and his son were surprised by a severe winter storm, a buffalo saved them from freezing to death.

The Snow Tipi was believed to have special healing powers — protecting those who lived in it from sickness and danger. It was also thought to bring bad weather, so it was seldom used in the summer camps when sunny weather was desired for hunting and working out of doors. The owners of painted tipis had major responsibilities for observing rituals and taboos that were part of the gift of the tipi design.

One day, many winters ago, Sacred Otter and his son were out hunting. They carried their bows in their hands and quivers of arrows on their backs, hoping to spot a herd of buffalo. They walked a long way before they heard or saw anything.

This was Blackfoot country, the open rolling hills of the Great Plains. Because it was winter, the grass was dry and brown. Although the sky above was bright and clear, near the western horizon it grew intense with gathering clouds.

Sacred Otter's son spotted a lone buffalo bull not too far away. The buffalo was big and fat and would provide food for the family for a great while. Both father and son watched it for some time to be sure it was not sickly. Before long, they both nocked arrows in their bows and shot at the same time, killing the old bull. As was their custom, they thanked the spirit of the buffalo and began at once to skin the hide from the carcass.

Intent on their work, they hardly noticed that the clouds were racing toward them with unusual speed. Soon the sky turned black with the wildly tumbling clouds, and a sharp, cold wind threatened.

Knowing they had no time to get back to Winter Camp, Sacred Otter and his son decided to cover themselves with the hide and the carcass of the buffalo they had just killed. Just in time, they crept inside the tiny refuge. The blizzard hit with furious force, soon covering the makeshift shelter, the man, and his son with deep snow. Yet, because snow is a good insulator, Sacred Otter and his son were kept warm and safe.

Soon Sacred Otter fell asleep and dreamed. In his dream, he saw a tipi he had never seen before. It was beautiful and very unusual. In his dream he walked around and around the tipi, looking at the decorations painted on the sides.

"Please come inside where it is warm, instead of walking around outside in the cold," said a voice.

Frightened, and cold from the storm, Sacred Otter opened the tipi flap and looked in. He saw a handsome old man sitting at the back of the tipi smoking a fine pipe. His hair was very long and so white that it shone in the dim light. He also wore a gleaming pure white robe.

"I am Estoneapesta, The Cold Maker. I bring snow, blizzards, and cold weather. This is my tipi," he said.

Sacred Otter quickly lost his fear, but he was so awestruck that he forgot his manners and could say very little. "It looks like a snow tipi," Sacred Otter said weakly.

"Indeed it is. I have named it Snow Tipi. I brought you and your son here to this place and sent the blizzard from the north," Cold Maker said sternly. "But because I pity your young son, I will spare your lives. I will also give you my Snow Tipi, my black stone pipe, and all the sacred power that goes along with these things."

Estoneapesta continued. "When you return to your people, make a new lodge, a fine big tipi, and paint it with symbols like those you see on mine."

Cold Maker then gave Sacred Otter prayers and songs to go with the ritual of the Snow Tipi. The ritual would be used in the winter for healing sickness. Last, Estoneapesta gave Sacred Otter a charm to wear on a leather thong around his neck. "This charm will protect you and those who live in the Snow Tipi from getting sick or being hurt."

Cold Maker gave Sacred Otter many instructions. He also described how to paint the Snow Tipi.

"You must paint the Snow Tipi yellow at the top because that is the color of the sunrise. The north wing must have the seven stars for the Great Bear because this is the direction from which I send blizzards. On the south wing paint the Bunched Stars [Pleiades]. At the back paint a large red circle to represent the sun. Attach a buffalo tail to the red sun. At all four directions where the lodge poles stand, place four claws for the thunderbird. Paint a wide yellow band at the bottom to represent the earth. On this yellow band put green circles, the color of ice. Hang horse tails on both sides of the door to ensure good horse hunting for the people. Finally, attach bunches of crow feathers and bells to the tops of the wing poles."

Then the maker of cold weather said farewell to Sacred Otter and departed. Sacred Otter awoke from his dream, and saw that the storm was almost gone. Sacred Otter knew that Cold Maker was leaving and was keeping his promise to save him and his son.

Sacred Otter and his son went back to Winter Camp and kept their secret until spring, the time when tipis were made. Then Sacred Otter kept his promise to Estoneapesta and built the first Snow Tipi, which he painted exactly as he had seen it in his dream.

As directed by Cold Maker, Sacred Otter made a leather pouch. Into this he placed the black stone pipe and the other items he had been given. This was the Snow Tipi sacred bundle. Sacred Otter hung the sacred bundle from a tripod at the front of the Snow Tipi, where it gave people a feeling of safety and comfort. However, at night or in bad weather, he took the sacred bundle inside the Snow Tipi to protect it.

On windy nights, it was particularly reassuring to hear the bells on the top of the Snow Tipi softly ringing in the wind as a promise from Cold Maker that the storms would not last forever and that his help and protection is always with the people.

> The Plains Indian tipi is a marvel of design, adapted to the restless life of a people who depended on their mobility to follow the vast herds of buffalo. Warm and comfortable in the fierce winter winds of the Plains and cool in the summer heat, the tipi was designed to be taken apart quickly and easily transported to the next campsite. There, it could be erected again in less than an hour. Though the tipi looks somewhat like an inverted ice cream cone, it is really shorter and steeper in the rear or west, to give it greater strength in the direction of the prevailing winds. This tilt also allows the smoke hole to be directly above the fire pit, which is to the east of the tipi's

center. The base of the tipi is egg-shaped to give it more width in the west. The small doorway faces toward the rising sun.

Tipi construction varied slightly among the tribes. The Blackfoot, Crow, and Hidatsa used four primary poles lashed together to support the remaining poles, while the Arapaho, Cheyenne, Kiowa, and Sioux used three. The Crow preferred very long poles, which extended high above the top of the tipi.

Among most tribes, the women traditionally fashioned their tipis out of wood, sinew rope, and buffalo skins. Every time the camp moved, it was the women who took the tipi down and erected it again in the new location. They cut the poles from long, slender pine or cedar trees, which they smoothed to make them easier to use. More than a hundred years ago, in the days when buffalo were still plentiful, the women sewed their tipi covers from buffalo skins provided by their husbands. They carefully tanned and sewed these skins together to make a supple, tight cover. After thoughtless white settlers and adventurers destroyed the great herds of buffalo, tipi covers were made of canvas.

The tipi required only two or three people to erect. In addition to the frame and skin cover, only hide ropes and wooden pegs were needed. About twenty poles, some twenty-five feet long, made up the wooden frame. First, three or four poles were tied together a few feet from the tips, and set up like a tripod to hold the remaining poles. One by one the rest of the poles were laid against this support and spread out to make the egg-shaped base. The skin cover was made up of twelve or more buffalo hides that were tanned, trimmed, and carefully sewn together with sinew thread. This cover was carefully spread out on the ground. Then, tying the last pole to the middle of the tipi cover, the women lifted the pole and cover into place against the west side of the framework. Next, the women stretched the cover around the tipi, bringing it together on the east side. They then pinned it together above and below the opening for the doorway with wooden pins. The last act of securing the tipi against high winds or inquisitive animals was to drive pegs into the ground every two feet or so through the bottom of the cover. When properly erected, the skin cover of a tipi was smooth and taut over the wooden framework.

The cover had two large flaps at the top of the cone to control the draft of the fire. Two poles, slightly shorter than the others, were placed into small pockets at the ends of the flaps and propped against the earth on the outside. These poles were used to control the size of the opening at the top of the tipi as weather conditions changed outside. When a new skin

tipi cover was made, its owner would light a smoky fire and close the tipi tight until the skin was thoroughly smoked. A smoked tipi cover would not harden when wet. A skin door, sometimes with the hair side out, was stretched across a hoop frame and tied to the frame and hide.

The tipi was remarkably comfortable year round. In the hot days of summer, the bottom of the tipi could be raised to allow the breeze to cool the interior. In the dead of winter, when fierce winter winds blew across the open prairie, grass, sod, or snow would be banked against the outside of the tipi where it was pegged to the earth. This provided extra warmth and cut down on drafts. The interior construction also assisted in climate control. An inner skin, called a "dew cloth," hung from a line tied around the inside several feet up from the bottom. This tanned buffalo hide, which was often decorated with pictures and war records, helped create a draft for the smoke from the open fire pit. It also kept any moisture from dripping off the framework onto the tipi's occupants. The family's bags of personal possessions were laid against the inner lining to help keep out cold air.

Early European travelers in the Plains often commented on how comfortable the tipi could be. Tipi dwellers slept on thick buffalo robes and walked on skin rugs spread over the grass. For sitting during the long winter nights of storytelling, or for entertaining, they also used comfortable willow frame backrests over which they hung robes or skins.

A few decades after the arrival of the Spanish in the Southwest and the Plains, the tribes began to use horses brought in by these newcomers to carry their belongings, especially the tipi cover and tipi poles. The long tipi poles were tied to the horses and pulled behind. Before they had the horse, the Plains people had to content themselves with using large dogs to carry their belongings while they walked with packs on their backs. Then, however, their hunting range was much smaller and their tipis smaller.

The constant traveling, and putting up and taking down the tipis shortened the poles and wore holes in the tipi cover. Every year, generally in the spring, both would have to be replaced. While the grassland of the Plains wakened from its long winter nap and renewed itself, the Plains women renewed their families' dwellings.

The Plains peoples, like most Native Americans, spent most of their time out of doors. The tipi lodge was used primarily for sleeping and for shelter from the weather. Within, each person in the household sat or slept in a place specified by tradition. For example, the oldest male generally slept on the far western side of the tipi. When sitting as a family or entertaining company, the men sat on the northern side of the tipi, and the women sat on the south. The oldest woman often slept beside the doorway to guard against dogs or other intruders. If the husband had more than one wife, each wife's sleeping place was defined by the household goods that belonged to her. Among most tribes, when entering a tipi, it is still proper to walk around to the left or south of the fire pit to reach your place, in the direction of the sun's path through the sky.

Clothes, dance regalia, and other important objects were often hung over "clothes lines" tied between the tipi poles. Cooking pots, parfleche bags with food, and firewood were stored near the entrance. Sacred medicine bundles, holding religious objects of great importance, might be tied high on the outside of the tipi or hung on tripods inside.

The Arapaho often hung beautifully prepared emblems outside their tipis. One type was a circular hide about eight inches across, embroidered with beads or porcupine quills. Two buffalo tails were attached to its center. It was sewed to the very top of the tipi on the west side opposite the door. Four similar, but smaller, circles were attached to the tipi a few feet from the bottom at the southeast, southwest, northwest, and northeast. In addition to a buffalo tail, these emblems had small pendants made of quill-wrapped sinew hanging from them. The Arapaho also attached pendants made of strings wrapped with quills to the sides of the doorway and to the ventilation flaps at the top of the tipi.

The embroidered disks were of three styles. The first carried alternating black and yellow concentric circles that represented the course Whirlwind Woman took in the time of the beginning when she assisted in making the earth. According to the Arapaho account of the beginning of the world, she was the first woman on earth. When earth was still small, Whirlwind Woman circled from place to place because she did not know where to stop and rest. By the time she stopped, she had whirled over the entire earth, and her circling had caused earth to grow ever larger until it reached the size it is today. Whirlwind Woman made the first tipi ornament, decorated like the ones on Arapaho tipis a hundred years ago. In addition to the concentric circles, she placed four lines radiating from the center to represent the four directions she traveled in her long journey.

Another style of disk, which represented the sun, was often beaded in four solid sectors rather than in bands. The sectors were red, the color of sunrise and sunset, and yellow, the color of the risen sun. From the center of the sun disk radiated four lines, which represented Morning Star, who rises just before the sun. Like the paintings on tipi covers, these emblems, though beautifully made, were sacred items and tied to the tipi to represent the Arapaho connection to the rest of the universe.

The Origin of the Buffalo Lodge

The Arapaho, like other Native American groups, have a number of sacred dances or ceremonies that they perform for the welfare of the people and to give thanks for the bounty of the watchful spirits. The Arapaho call their ceremonial dances "lodges," because they are held in a lodge-like enclosure. For each lodge there is a story describing its origin. The Buffalo Lodge of a century ago was a woman's ceremony, which was held in part to assure success in providing food for the band that held it.

Holding a ceremonial dance is a sacred trust and a task that one does not commit to lightly. The woman who pledged to hold a Buffalo Ceremony did so in full knowledge that it would require resources of goods and time, and most of all a willing heart. She had to persuade other women both to participate in the ceremony and to contribute food and ceremonial regalia.

The Buffalo Lodge itself was made of tipi poles and skins contributed by the people of the camp. The preparers of the ceremony tied seven tipi poles together near the top with a buffalo-skin rope. Horizontally across they tied a digging stick painted red. Against the digging stick they rested other tipi poles. A pole at the northeast and one in the southwest were painted black to represent the night. One in the northwest and one in the southeast were painted red to represent day. Finally, they attached several tipi skins to the poles, leaving an entrance in the east. The Buffalo Ceremony itself was a series of sacred dances that lasted a total of six days.

In the following story, as the tribe travels from one camp circle to the next, it leaves a poor family along the trail to fend for itself. Although the family is poor in material wealth, each family member has a good heart and is rich in respect and caring for others, traits that are rewarded by Buffalo Cow.

A long time in the past a man and his wife watched their tribe move slowly out of sight over the next hill because they could not keep up. They were left alone with five children to care for. The family was so poor it had only one pony to carry its tipi and children. But their pony had become lame and now limped so slowly that they had fallen ever farther behind the rest of the tribe.

Evening fell heavily on the young family, but they could still appreciate the peaceful and beautiful scenery. They had rested in a clump of sycamore trees near a stream. The surrounding grass was thick and the air was fresh. On the horizon to the north, mountains rose out of the low rolling hills in a faint purple haze. To the west, the mountains were near and steep.

"We cannot go much farther tonight," the man said to his weary wife. "Why don't we rest here?"

She looked up at him as she nursed their baby daughter. "This looks like a sweet and plentiful place to set up camp for the night," she said.

"There are deer tracks and rabbit prints, and the bushes are heavy with berries," he said hopefully. "At least we will not starve here."

"Perhaps we will find fresh game tomorrow." She put the baby down and began to unpack the pony.

"We would not be alone if our people had given us a little help," said the husband with a sigh. "But they just left us," he mused, as he helped his wife pitch their thin, patched tipi by the creek.

The next day the man set out in search of game. Although he saw many deer along his way, without a horse, he could not approach within shooting range. He came home to the little tipi empty-handed and told his wife about the many deer he had seen. She prepared a meal for the family with their remaining food.

She said, "We cannot hope to catch up with our people now. Why don't we set up permanent camp here and make do with what we can gather from this bountiful land?"

They did just that. Their pony was happy because there was such good grass. He was becoming fatter by the day and his lame leg was healing quickly.

Each day the husband set out for deer and each day he would see plenty of game. Yet each day, he could not get close enough to shoot. He came home empty-handed again and again.

His wife had better luck. She and their eldest daughter were able to catch an occasional rabbit, pick berries, and dig enough roots to make a hearty stew for dinner. This, with the sparkling water from the stream, sustained them for many days.

As autumn drew near, yellow leaves appeared on the trees along the creek-bed. Days grew shorter and the air took on a crisp edge. It was on one of these days that the hopeful hunter came upon a buffalo cow and her calf, grazing on the thick, dry grass along the path he took when going hunting.

"What a lucky day," he thought to himself. "This buffalo cow is so old and slow that I am sure to be able to shoot her."

Carefully and slowly he crept closer to the old buffalo cow. Just as he came within shooting range, Buffalo Cow turned toward him and spoke. "Listen to me!"

The hunter was so surprised that he could do nothing. She spoke again.

"Listen to me, Man! I have watched you and your wife every day and find you both worthy, good hearted, and dedicated to the land. I have seen your respect and want you to help your people. Unlike your tribe, I take pity on you and will help you. But you must do exactly as I say."

Buffalo Cow walked closer and gave him very clear and detailed instructions, which he agreed to follow.

"Cut dogwood branches for one hundred arrows and have your wife cut poles and gather all the firewood that she can. Stack the wood along the side of the tipi," Buffalo Cow said. "Do what I tell you, and I will reveal sacred things to you."

Without further delay, he hurried home to his family. His wife had caught another rabbit that morning and the aroma of a hearty stew reached him as he came near the creek. He did not tell her about the buffalo cow and calf but did give her instructions about cutting poles and gathering firewood.

Each day that autumn was much like the others. The husband cut, peeled, straightened, and feathered dogwood sticks for arrows. The wife cut poles, as instructed by Buffalo Cow, and gathered firewood. She stacked the firewood on all sides of the tipi to act as a windbreak in case of a snowstorm. He made a strong bow for his arrows.

In time, all was made ready as Buffalo Cow had instructed. "Listen to me, my wife," he said, "I am going to lie down and dream. If you see or hear anything unusual, be brave and act courageous." He tied the hundred arrows in a bundle and leaned back on them to go to sleep.

He dreamed until dawn. And in his vision, Buffalo Cow revealed many things to him.

At first daylight, his wife heard a great noise like hundreds of footsteps outside the tipi. She looked out and saw that it had snowed that night. She also saw Buffalo Cow at the tipi door and a huge herd of buffalo beyond her. For a moment she stood amazed but remembered what her husband had told her. She did not shout or run away in fear. She woke her husband and told him to look outside.

"Behold our sustenance for the future," he whispered quietly. He fired arrow after arrow until he had used all one hundred arrows. He was able to kill a hundred buffalo. "Let the rest of the herd stand a way off, just far enough for me to see," he told the leader of the buffalo herd. They retreated about four or five miles down the plains. "And now, my wife, we must get busy. The One Above has pitied us."

All that day and many others, the whole family worked to prepare the meat — slicing it and hanging it on poles to dry. After all the meat was done, the wife began working on the hides — scraping and tanning them. She also gathered poles to build a Buffalo Lodge, for now she had seen her husband's vision also.

When this was done, she melted fat for tallow, mixed the best roasted meat with it, and added sweet berries. She mixed it all together to make a sweet pemmican. She packed the pemmican in the lining of the buffalo intestine and tied the ends tightly. When she was finished, she called him to see.

"Good! That is the right thing to do," he exclaimed. "I will pack it all tomorrow and take it with me."

The next morning, he packed it on his back and trudged off to search for the camp of his people to tell them of his vision and the sacred knowledge he had learned from Buffalo Cow.

After many days, he arrived at the camp of his people and asked for the chief's tipi. When he had been made welcome, he brought out his bundle of pemmican and shared it with everyone. But as much as they took, and they took much because they were starving, the pemmican in the bundle never decreased. The people were amazed.

Then the man told the people of his land of plenty. He told of his vision and the promises of Buffalo Cow. The old chief thought for a time. Then he told his people to prepare for a journey to this new land.

When they arrived at the new place, the man told them that he had something important to say. The people all gathered to listen.

"It is very important to change the way you have been living so there can be peace and plenty in the land and among our peoples. First of all, my wife has already begun to build a Buffalo Lodge. This lodge will benefit all the people. Ceremonies will be held in the Lodge so that Buffalo Cow's promise of health will continue. Only in this way can the power of the promise continue with us."

The old men of the camp were also given insight into his vision. They now knew that only by respecting the land, helping each other, and caring for the sick and needy could the people continue to live. The old men were told of the sacred dances and began the Buffalo Lodge Society.

Part of their vision came as instructions for making a sacred bundle that should hang in the Buffalo Lodge and become a part of the rituals. In this sacred bundle were bear claws, buffalo horns, rattles, buffalo tails, paint, tallow, and special sacred stones.

The old men priests hung the bundle in the center of the tipi. The Buffalo Lodge was in the center of the camp and remains there to this day.

8 Models of the World
Pawnee Earth Lodges

Not all Plains tribes made the portable tipi their permanent home. The so-called "village tribes" from the north central Plains once lived in large, comfortable earth lodges, especially during the spring and summer. These Indian groups included the Arikara, Hidatsa, and Mandan, along the Missouri River to the north; the Omaha, Oto, and Ponca to the east; and the Pawnee in the mid-Plains. For most of these tribes, the summer earth lodge was central to their life and religion.

The village tribes settled along the streams and rivers to fish and to grow corn, beans, squash, watermelon, and tobacco. The crops they grew brought to their villages other, more nomadic, Plains tribes who traded shells, trinkets, and other exotic goods from far away for produce. Some trade routes extended as far west as the Pacific Ocean and as far east as the Appalachians. Because the settlements were generally located on high bluffs along the river, they were visible for miles around.

By the time Europeans encountered these tribes in the eighteenth century, their villages were already major trade centers. These first European visitors marveled at the orderly arrangement of the villages and at the spaciousness and comfort of the lodges. They also praised the hospitable nature of the villagers, who took pride in making their European visitors comfortable.

The village tribes used tipis for short hunting trips in the summer or for longer buffalo hunts in the fall and winter. Some groups also constructed smaller winter earth lodges in protected areas in the forests where they could easily gather firewood. Some moved back into their summer home. Nevertheless, they all considered the summer earth lodge their true home.

The earth lodge was especially important to the Pawnee, who lived along the Platte and the Loop Rivers in what has since become Kansas and Nebraska. The largest of the Pawnee bands was the Skidi Band. During the eighteenth century the Pawnee lived in villages of from ten to fifteen lodges. Each lodge housed up to thirty or forty family members. For their food, the Pawnee depended about equally on the vegetables and fruits from their gardens and meat from buffalo hunts.

By the end of the nineteenth century, the villages and the earth lodge had all but disappeared as the Skidi and other Pawnee bands fell victim to European diseases, harassment by the nearby Sioux, and the pressures of white settlers moving into their traditional homelands. The disappearance of the buffalo, one of their staple foods, hastened the end of the Pawnee's traditional way of life. In 1875, the United States government forcibly moved the few remaining Pawnee to a reservation in Oklahoma. The last known Pawnee earth lodge was built there in 1905 and was used for ceremonies.

The Morning Star Bundle

The Skidi believed that each of their villages was created by a star or group of stars. Each village kept and treasured a sacred bundle, said to have been given by the founding star. The bundle was the focus of the village's ceremonial life and was made up of the objects needed to perform the sacred rituals connected with the bundle. Sacred bundles might carry meteorites, paint, animal skins, and other objects. The meteorites were considered especially important because they came from the sky and were thought to be children of Tirawahat that have flown down from heaven. The following Skidi myth of one of the sacred bundles is notable for its stone lodge, and for the coyote skin that was used in the Morning Star bundle.

In the days when people were being created, Tirawahat, The One Above, decided to give them sacred bundles. The bundles would help people conduct ceremonies and make prayers to the stars.

He was not sure how to reach the people so he asked the two Morning Stars to be his intermediaries on earth. They agreed to transform themselves into old men and live near the people. Because they were stars, they could not see in the daytime. Hence, as men they would be blind during the day.

Tirawahat and the Morning Stars talked a long time about the sort of house they should have. Since they were going to be blind they needed strong shelter that would keep out intruders. Finally they decided that a stone lodge would be best because it would be safer to live in than a tipi or an earth lodge, but much more pleasant than a cave or a hollow log.

The stone lodge Tirawahat gave them looked much like an earth lodge. It was a large mound with an entrance in the east. It also had an opening in the top to let smoke escape. Inside, however, it had no supporting posts, as none were necessary for a stone lodge. Whenever the two blind men wanted to go in or out, all they had to do was say to the stone that covered the doorway, "Grandfather, move." Then the stone door would move far enough to allow one man at a time to leave or enter. When they wanted it to close, they said, "Grandfather, close."

The two brothers came down to earth and became blind. Each brought a bundle with him that he hung in the lodge. On either side of the bundles, they placed a spear in case anyone tried to enter their stone lodge. They set up housekeeping and, as they were now men, cooked and ate meat.

One day Coyote was loping along, looking here and there for something to eat, when he saw a crow flying by, a large piece of meat in his beak. "Grandchild," Coyote called, "where did you find that meat? It looks delicious." To Coyote anything to eat looks delicious.

"Yes, it's wonderful. I found it close by. If you are here tomorrow at the same time, I will show you where," said Crow.

The next day, Coyote appeared and Crow took him to a stone hill. It was the lodge of the Morning Stars. Crow and Coyote sat down on the top, where they could look into the stone lodge through the smoke hole.

"Two blind men live in this stone lodge. Just watch, and in a little while one of them will reach into a parfleche bag filled with dried buffalo meat. He will put the meat into the pot hanging over the fireplace and cook it. When the meat is done, he will cut it into pieces and divide it equally with his partner in two wooden bowls."

Coyote watched carefully, and soon it was as Crow had said. "Now watch me," said Crow. When the meat was in the wooden bowls, Crow flew down through the hole in the roof and grabbed a small piece of meat from one of the bowls. He flew up to the roof and gave the piece to Coyote, who wolfed it down greedily. Crow then flew in again and stole a piece for himself. Coyote wanted more, so Crow took several more pieces. After they had eaten all they could that day, Crow flew home. But Coyote decided to stay right there on the side of that stone lodge and make his home where he could see Crow fly by.

Each day, when it was dinner time for the two old men, Coyote would watch for Crow and meet him near the hole of the roof. One day, Coyote was hungrier than usual and grew impatient waiting for Crow to steal the meat for him. "Help me get down there Crow. Then I'll be able to get my own food. I can't always be waiting for you."

Crow agreed, but warned, "You may find it hotter than you wish. How will you get out again?"

"I'll think of something," replied Coyote.

Crow took him down into the lodge by grabbing Coyote's ears in his beak and gliding in. Then Crow flew back to the top, leaving Coyote in the lodge.

Coyote was greedy, and could not wait for the meat to be cut into small pieces. As soon as one of the blind men put a piece of meat in his friend's wooden bowl, Coyote grabbed it and scampered away.

"I thought you said you put meat in my bowl," said one.

"I did," said the other. "I gave you a piece just as large as the one in my bowl. Here, you can feel in my bowl." The second old man handed the first his own bowl. But before the first was able to feel it, Coyote stole that piece of meat, too.

"You are just playing with me. There's no meat in your bowl either. You must have eaten it already."

"No, I didn't. You must have stolen both pieces for yourself."

The two old men began to argue and to accuse each other of being overly greedy. Coyote began to worry. Soon they may figure out that I stole their meat, he thought. I can't call to Crow, or they'll hear me. Perhaps if I can get them fighting with each other, I can find a way to escape.

Coyote sneaked in close to one of them and hit him hard on the side of the face with his paw. Then he motioned to Crow to come down and carry him out again. But Crow just laughed and settled back to watch the fun.

"Why did you hit me?" said the old man.

"I didn't hit you. I'm way over here."

Coyote came around to the second old man and hit him too, right across the face with his paw.

"Ow! There was no need to strike me, brother," complained the second one.

"I didn't hit you, you fool."

"Who else could have? Besides, I could feel the hair on your hand."

"The hair on my hand is nearly gone from old age. But now that you mention it, the hand that struck me was hairy, too. There must be somebody in here, some animal, causing us to fight so. After all, we are good friends."

"Yes, I believe you're right. It must be Coyote. Let us take our spears and see if we can catch him. You go toward the east. I will go toward the west."

The two then assumed fighting positions and began sticking their spears into the side of the lodge, hoping to strike the intruder. Coyote worked hard to dodge their spears, for even blind, these old brothers knew how to hunt. He grew so tired jumping out of their way that he began to pant. Then they heard him and were able to follow his motions by ear. Finally one of the spears struck Coyote. After one loud yelp, he died.

One old man then said, "We lack one thing in our bundle — a coyote quiver to hold arrows for a bow." The other agreed and they began immediately to skin Coyote. Throwing away his carcass, they kept the hide. After tanning and drying it, they made it into a quiver. Now the sacred bundle was complete.

Several hours later, one of the men approached the stone doorway, saying, "Grandfather, move." The stone door moved aside and the man went out into the night. He walked until he came to the nearby village and found a certain young boy sleeping in the lodge with his parents. He brought the boy, who was still asleep, to the stone lodge. When he reached the lodge, he commanded the stone, "Grandfather, close," and the stone moved back into place.

The two men awakened the boy and told him that they had brought him there to teach him the secrets of the bundle. The boy stayed with the men many years, helping them and learning the ceremony of the bundle. After he had learned all he could, they told him to take the bundle back to the village and to hold the ceremonies once a year.

The two old men stayed on in the stone lodge until it was time to return to the heavens and take their places by the side of Tirawahat. From then on, some of the sacred bundles had coyote quivers in them.

The First Earth Lodge

Sacred stories and rituals guided most of Pawnee life. According to their beliefs, in the beginning the most powerful Pawnee god, Tirawahat, created the universe. Then he chose the location of the very first earth lodge. It was built as a home for the first children, who became the mother and the father of the Pawnee people. The first girl was born of the marriage of Morning and Evening Star. The first boy came from the union of Sun and Moon.

Tirawahat chose a site in which a great ash tree was growing. The ash tree became the center of the lodge. In one version of the story, the stars descended from the sky and placed the posts that were later to represent them. The central fireplace was made by the stars called the Circle of Chiefs (Corona Borealis), who burned the ash tree in the center of the lodge.

The god Paruxti, the Wonderful Being, who was spokesman for Tirawahat, taught the Pawnee people how to build their lodges. Paruxti lived in a lodge in the west and made himself known to the people in the form of Wind, Cloud, Lightning, and Thunder.

The earth lodge enclosed and protected the people within and provided them with sacred power from the gods of the sky. In the daytime, Sun sent down his warmth through the open smoke hole to light the interior. At night, the stars above offered their protective powers. Even many of the lodge's furnishings represented sacred power. For example, the Pawnee considered their two most important foods, buffalo and corn, to be sacred. In some houses, an altar on the west side of the lodge opposite the doorway held a buffalo skull and a sacred bundle of objects that included ears of corn. According to Pawnee sacred stories, the altar represented the garden of Evening Star where the first corn was grown in the beginning of the world.

In the long winter nights, with their children and relatives warm and snug before them in the comfortable earth lodge, Pawnee elders told stories of the beginning of the world and how the Pawnee people came to be. They also reminded their listeners of the sacred nature of the earth lodge and how new ones were to be built. This story comes from the Chaui Band of the Pawnee, and describes in detail the building of the earth lodge.

Paruxti, Tirawahat's spokesman, told the people, "I will show you how to build a proper lodge so you will stay warm and dry in the winter and cool in the summer. First, gather timber from the forests and cut ten strong forked poles. They will support the lodge. Dig ten holes in a large circle and set each pole into the ground. Then gather many straight poles to lay across the forked ones," he said.

"Place four of the largest upright poles like the corners of a long box. The long sides should extend to the east and west." Paruxti explained the meaning of these poles: "They must be strong in order to hold up the heavy roof of the lodge. They represent the four gods who hold up the heaven in the northeast, southeast, northwest, and southwest. The weaker poles between represent the lesser gods. The lodge must always face east toward the rising Sun and Morning Star, so it can breathe.

"Then set up an outer circle of poles for the many other gods, and link them together with roof poles, just as the gods extend their power from one to another." Paruxti continued his instructions, telling the people that the north side of the lodge should be for the women and the south side for the men. "Net supple willow branches together and place them on the sides of the lodge. They symbolize the ribs of the gods of the four directions.

"When you have completed the framework," he continued, "and covered it with earth from Mother Earth, dig a fire pit in the center and carry the dirt outside and heap it on a mound just beyond the entranceway. Each day when Sun rises, he will see that mound."

Paruxti then told the people that he would give them firesticks, which belong to the sun, so they could make fires to cook their food. "When you level the ground within the lodge, leave a small pile of dirt in the west for an altar. On this altar, place the skull of a freshly killed buffalo." Paruxti promised the people that the spirit of the buffalo, the spirit of Tirawahat himself, would always live in the skull. "So keep the skull on the altar at all times, facing east. I will also give you a sacred bundle to hang on the wall over the altar."

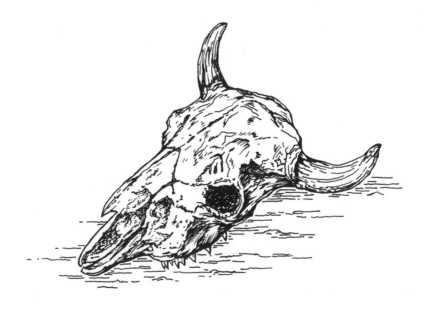

"The women will be in charge of the bundle, which contains a pipe, tobacco, mother-corn, and painted sticks with scalps taken in earlier battles attached. Keep the bundle open so all can see what is in it and keep four painted sticks outside the lodge, one in each of the four directions to honor the principal gods.

"Listen to the voice of Tirawahat your Father, the Thunder, and give gifts to him and to the other gods.

"Now I make special gifts to men and to women. To men I give a bow and arrows. To women I also give a bow and arrows, a hoe, and seeds of red, yellow, black, and white corn. These things will provide your sustenance."

Paruxti continued. "Know this. The earth lodge represents Mother Earth. The lodge itself is her breast, the smoke from the cooking fire being pulled up into the smoke hole is like milk being pulled from a mother's breast by her baby. The fireplace where you do your cooking acts like a mother's breast, giving you food that will make you strong. All things of the earth represent Mother Earth, and all heavenly things represent your Sun Father.

"Remember these things, keep them in your hearts, and pass them down from generation to generation to your children, so they will live in harmony with earth and with the heavens, with the peoples and with the gods. Then you will prosper and grow strong."

> The earth lodge, which might extend 45 feet across and 18 feet high, was entered by walking down a long tunnel-like entranceway. The floor was as much as three feet below ground level. Because the entrance faced east or southeast, in the morning, rays from the rising sun would stream down the long opening and fall on the buffalo altar opposite. In the summer, sunlight would come from the northeast; in the winter from the southeast.
>
> Growing up in a Pawnee lodge was a special experience. While providing shelter from the sun's heat, rain, and wind, the parts of the lodge continually reminded the family of the form of the sky and earth, and the spiritual forces that made them. It helped the young people living in it to understand the

world outside and to feel at home in the cosmos.

The lodge was a place to live but, because it was sacred, the Pawnee also held their ceremonies in the lodge. To determine the proper time to begin these ceremonies, the Pawnee priests watched for the appearance of certain stars through the smoke hole at the top of the lodge.

One of the most important ceremonies of the year was the Thunder Ritual, which marked the beginning of the Pawnee year. It was held when Thunder, which was thought to be the voice of Paruxti, began to be heard in the spring. Yet isolated bursts of thunder might be heard at any time, so to be sure they were holding the ceremony at the proper time, the priests watched for the star pattern they called the Seven Stars (Pleiades) to appear in the right position in the smoke hole. They also waited for the first appearance of two stars they called the Swimming Ducks, which lie at the tail of the constellation Scorpio. The appearance of Swimming Ducks, and the lightning and thunder that soon arrived, told them that the long winter was over.

As soon as possible after the first thunder was heard, following the first appearance of Swimming Ducks, a lodge was selected to hold the ceremony. The floor was swept, any unnecessary furniture removed, and the fireplace cleaned. The old ashes were dumped just east of the door. The priests could then proceed with the Thunder Ritual, which prompted the health and well-being of the Pawnee people and instructed them in their duties toward the gods. Most important, it prepared the people spiritually for the agricultural ceremonies that followed soon after, and the buffalo rites later in the summer and fall.

James R. Murie, who was born in 1862 of a Pawnee mother and a Scots father, became extremely interested in the ceremonies of the Pawnee people. Murie spent many years talking with the elders of his tribe and learning their ancient lore and ritual. It is from him that we have much of the detailed information about Pawnee ritual and about the earth lodge. The following is his short and eloquent statement about the meaning of the earth lodge:

> The simple dwelling is full of beauty to him who knows its meaning. There is no part of it that is not symbolic. The entrance must always face the rising sun, the round domed roof is a symbol of the sky, and each post represents a star which tells the Pawnee of some divine being. So whether within his walls or upon the open prairie the Pawnee lived in conscious recognition of the universe about him, even in the presence of Tirawahat, the One Above.
>
> — Quoted in Von Del Chamberlain,
> *When Stars Came Down to Earth*, p. 155

9 The Big House
A *Delaware Ceremonial Dwelling*

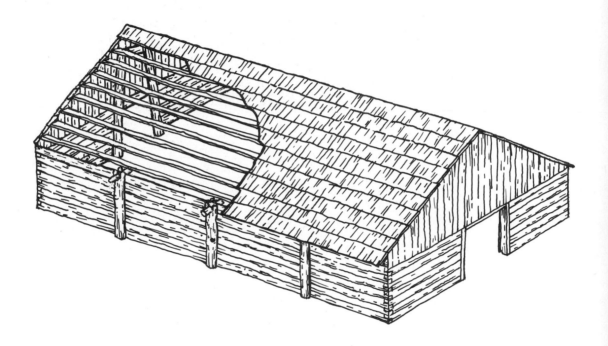

Originally the Indian bands that call themselves Lenape Indians lived in the Delaware River valley on land that is now part of the states of Delaware, New Jersey, New York, and Pennsylvania. White settlers gave them the name Delaware after the English name of the Delaware River.

What little is known about the daily lives of the Delaware before they began to move away from the East Coast was gathered by early European explorers and settlers. The Delaware lived in small villages of no more than a few hundred persons. They never became a single political unit like the

Iroquois, but were loosely connected with each other in a network of alliances. These alliances were formed to promote a common defense against outside enemies and to govern the use of shared resources, like the oyster beds of Delaware Bay. The Delaware grew corn and tobacco in small fields, and gathered fruits and nuts that grew in the substantial forests of their homeland. These same forests provided deer and other animals. Fishing and shellfishing along streams and in Delaware Bay supplied additional sustenance.

Their houses were a variety of size and shape, but those best described by early explorers were the multifamily longhouses that might be as long as a hundred feet and as wide as twenty feet. Hickory saplings formed the house frames. They were set in the ground in pairs and tied together to form an arch. Long sections of chestnut bark were tied to the frames for siding. Temporary dwellings near the cornfields, or close to hunting and fishing grounds, sheltered the bands in the summer.

In the eighteenth and nineteenth centuries white settlements pushed the Delaware bands westward into western Pennsylvania, Ohio, Canada, and eventually to Oklahoma, where they have become assimilated into Euro-American culture.

The Big House Ceremony

During the early 1800s, hard pressed by white settlers who wanted their land and dispersed by the soldiers who kept pushing them farther from their homeland, the Delaware bands looked for any means of relief. A woman prophet named Beate arose among the Munsee band. She urged her people to combine their various celebrations into a single ceremony, held in October and lasting twelve days. The home of the new celebration was the Big House, deliberately built without the use of glass windows, iron nails, or other European materials.

The Big House was thought of as a miniature universe. Each of the four walls symbolized one of the four grandparents of the Lenape creation story: The floor was the earth. The roof was the heavens. The central post, which carried carved images of the game spirits, linked the lower worlds, earth, and sky. The dance floor, where the Delaware men and women danced and prayed and shared their visions, represented the Milky Way, which the Delaware called the Beautiful White Path.

The Big House Ceremony began long ago when the earth began to quake in the land where the Delawares lived. The earth shook greatly, and terrible rumbling noises were heard everywhere. Gigantic cracks appeared on the surface of the earth; steam, dust, and smoke hissed from the fissures, and a thick, foul, black liquid that looked like tar oozed out from the underworld. All the animals and people were terrified.

Even to this day, no one knows what this substance was. They say it came from the Evil Manitou, who breathed it forth.

All of the Delaware men gathered together to decide what to do with this threat to their lives and well-being. One after another, the men began to tell what they had dreamed or heard.

"We have angered the Great Manitou by not praying to him and giving thanks for what we have," one man said.

"We have need of a ceremony," said another.

"But first we need to build a Big House in which to pray and hold a great yearly ceremony," another urged.

"My dream told me how big the house should be and how it should look on the outside," added still another man.

One man dreamed of the doors — one facing the rising sun, another facing the setting sun. Another dreamed of the large center posts on which he saw two sacred carvings of a human face — one facing east and the other facing west. Smaller sacred carved faces he saw on each of the four doorposts and on each of the six posts that supported the sides of the Big House of his dream. One side of each of the twelve faces was painted red, and the other side was painted black.

The Big House was very special and was to be used only once a year for the Delaware Annual Ceremony. The ceremony itself should last for twelve days. The people would recite visions, pray for all people, and for the whole earth. They would also hear the myths retold. All of this and more was told to the men in dreams.

"We must choose officers for the ceremony each year," one man was told in his dreams, "three men and three women. These six officers will do most of the work and will keep the peace."

Following the instructions of the dreams, the men built the first Big House and held the first ceremony. The earthquakes stopped. The people knew that if they stopped holding the ceremony, the earthquakes and other, even more horrible, things would begin happening all over again.

> Then, as in later days, the six officers were the first to arrive at the Big House before the annual ceremony. It was their duty and their honor to prepare the building for the ceremony.
>
> The men would repair any damage and fill holes in the walls with mortar. The women swept and dusted the building. The men cut wood for the ceremonial fires and the women cleaned the huge pots used for the hominy that was cooked and eaten during the ceremonial feast.
>
> A great fire was laid in the fireplace. The first ceremonial fire was lit using an old fire-drill, a pointed stick that was twirled rapidly against a dry piece of wood to create enough heat to start a fire. The men guarded the outside of the Big House and the women swept both sides of the fire twelve times, sweeping a road to heaven.

When all the preparations were complete, the attendants called the people inside to begin the ceremony. The chief would invite people to pray, each in his or her own way. Visions would be recited by those so gifted. There was feasting, and peace and order would be restored to the Delaware and to the world for yet another year.

As one Delaware said about their ceremony:

"The people could get along fine, if they followed the rules of the meeting — not only the Delawares, but the other people round about. For when the Delaware prays, he prays for things that will benefit everybody; he prays for the children as well as for himself; he prays for future time. But if anything comes to destroy the world, it will be too late to think of starting the Big House then."

It is said by some that earthquakes and terrible disruptions in the weather began to occur once again when the Delaware stopped holding the Big House Ceremony. The last complete Big House Ceremony was held in Oklahoma in 1924.

10 The First Sweatlodge

Native American groups throughout North America build sweathouses, or sweatlodges, to heal themselves and to purify their bodies and their spirits. Sweating is one way in which our bodies rid themselves of various salts and of germs that cause illness. A prolonged sweat, followed up by a dip in cold water or a vigorous rubdown with sand and herbs, cleans and invigorates. Although the sweatlodge ritual is not as common as it once was, Native Americans still use this ritual to promote health.

The special qualities of the sweat bath give it great religious significance. For many tribes, the sweat bath is an important part of their ceremonies. During the sweat bath, participants pray to be purified and to receive strength and good fortune. They believe that the life-giving power of the universe works through the sweat bath to heal them, or to give them the spiritual strength they need to accomplish difficult tasks.

Some sweatlodges are made from a simple stick frame and covered over with hides. Others are more elaborate and are constructed of wood, or logs and earth. The sweatlodge is deeply revered. It is never made in haste or without saying prayers that the effort would please the spirits who watch over the people.

Chief Sweatlodge

The Sanpoil Indians of what is now central Washington state thought of their sweatlodge as both a place of healing and as a guardian spirit. They built their sweatlodge from a framework of arches made by pounding both ends of flexible birch or willow branches into the ground. These they covered with bark and grass and, finally, with earth. If the sweatlodge was a temporary one, built, for example, near a summer encampment, they would cover the framework with skins or blankets. They always placed the sweatlodge entrance so it opened toward a nearby stream or lake.

As in sweatlodge ceremonies throughout North America, the Sanpoil heated stones outside the sweatlodge and rolled or carried them into the center of the lodge, where they sprinkled them with water. The steam that rose from the hot stones heated the lodge and carried the bathers' prayers upward to the spirit of the sweatlodge. After sweating, they would plunge into the nearby stream or lake, to refresh themselves. In this story, Chief Sweatlodge is both a sweatlodge and creator of the Sanpoil and their world.

A very long time ago, before things were established as they are now, there lived a great Chief who decided to create and name the birds and animals. When he was finished, he looked at each of his new creations proudly and called them all together. He stood before them and spoke.

"Before long, people will be created. They will have children and their children, children. The people will send their children out to listen to you, and you will tell them what they can become when they grow up."

At this point, the Chief paused and looked around at all the birds and animals assembled before him. They all waited attentively for him to continue.

"You must tell the boy children," Chief continued, "that they will become good husbands, fathers, fishermen, hunters, and leaders. You will tell the girl children that they are to be wives, mothers, healers, and peacekeepers."

An old eagle looked at him and asked, "And what will you become, Chief, when these new people are come?"

Chief spoke again and said, "I will become Sweatlodge for any who choose to construct me. The one who builds me can pray to me and I will give him what he wishes. If he wishes good looks or good fortune, I will help guide him. If he is sick or injured, I will help heal him. If he is sad or lonely, I will console him. If he is dying, I will help him to see the world that is to come. My name will be Sweatlodge from now on and I will help the new people."

Blue Jay and Sweatlodge

The Thompson Indians of British Columbia lived in the river valleys, hunting, fishing, and gathering berries, herbs, and other plants. In the cold winter months, several families lived together in unusual, large, round houses, which extended below ground. To make their winter house, the Thompson Indians sank four heavy posts firmly in the ground, leaning toward one another, one pair along a line from the northeast to the southwest and the other between the southeast and northwest. Rafters tied to these posts supported smaller logs, which were tightly tied in a framework and covered over with pine needles and earth. Occupants entered and exited these snug, warm houses by means of a notched-log ladder that extended through the roof's smoke hole. The top of the ladder was often carved with the head of a bird or animal and then painted.

In the warm weather the Thompson Indians lived in much lighter summer lodges made from a log framework covered with mats or bark. Their sweathouses were very similar to those of the Sanpoil — a simple framework covered with blankets. In their tales, Blue Jay was a comic character who always acted like a clown. The following story contrasts the comic Blue Jay with Sweathouse, a serious old man who always looks after the people's welfare.

In the ancient days, Blue Jay and his relative Sweathouse lived with the people and were men. In the daytime, Sweathouse took the form of a bent cedar pole

of the sweathouse and watched the people. In the night, he resumed his normal form of a bent old man and wandered about.

Blue Jay hid from the people, much as he does today. He was the greatest trickster of the ancients, always joking and making fun of the people. Then, as now, he would sit in a tree and imitate voices of other birds. He would also imitate the voices of the people to coax them near. When they would come under his tree, he would swoop down, shrieking at them and frightening them. However, he could not tolerate being made fun of himself. If anyone dared to make fun of him, he would sulk and pout. His mouth would become distorted and twisted.

After a long, long time, the people grew tired of Blue Jay and his pranks. They decided to move away, hoping Blue Jay would get bored and lonely and find somewhere else to live.

The people moved about for four summers and four winters, living in different places according to the weather. Certain that they had been away long enough that Jay was now gone, they returned to their old home. Imagine their surprise to find Blue Jay still there — still making trouble. Sadly but with determination, they left their old home for good, taking all their belongings to another country. Blue Jay and Sweathouse were left alone.

One day Old-One, a Transformer, came along and found Sweathouse and Blue Jay all alone and the people gone. Old-One turned Blue Jay into a squawking, chattering bird. "You will be a copy-cat and mocker forever, only imitating the sounds of other birds and animals," he told Blue Jay harshly. "You will never be taken seriously."

Then Old-One turned to Sweathouse. "From now on, you will be the spirit of the sweathouse. The people will come to you for comfort and for healing and will pray to you. You will be very powerful and be able to help the people and to grant their most earnest prayers." And so it was.

The First Sweatlodge

The Navajo and the Apache brought the sweatlodge to the Southwest centuries ago when they migrated there from the north. Both tribes still make active use of the structure for ceremonial purposes. Only men construct the sweatlodge, singing special songs appropriate for building it. By tradition, it must be put together in less than a day.

The Navajo sweatlodge resembles a small five-log hogan, but without a smoke hole. Most are only large enough to hold one person at a time. The bather must crawl through the doorway and squat down on his heels to be comfortable. Builders use juniper or spruce logs for the framework.

First they dig a shallow, round pit some six to eight feet across to serve as the sweatlodge floor. Next, three forked logs are placed in the earth a foot or so beyond the edge of the pit, one each in the south, west, and north, leaning against one another for support. Finally, the builders sink two poles in the earth toward the east to make a doorway. They use small sticks and brush to fill in between the poles and then cover the entire framework with dirt. When the sweatlodge is used for ceremonials, it is often painted with a ritual sandpainting of a rainbow, lightning, or a sunbeam.

After the basic structure is complete, the owner may cover the floor with juniper bark, spruce twigs, or sagebrush. He then gathers about a dozen large, rounded sandstone rocks to use in warming the interior. These are heated in a fire just outside the entrance and carried inside between two sticks. When the sweatlodge is in use, the doorway is covered with four blankets, hides, or canvas. The heated stones are most often used dry, but sometimes a little water may be thrown on

 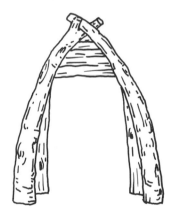

to create steam. After the heated rocks become too cracked from continually being heated and cooled, they are piled up outside on the northwest side of the sweatlodge and replaced with new rocks.

Families who keep the traditional ways will nearly always have a sweatlodge somewhere near their hogan, generally located in a secluded place sheltered from public view. Often it is situated near a source of water so users can bathe afterward. If water is unavailable, they place the sweatlodge near a sandy wash so they can dry off by rolling in the sand.

The Navajo tell several different versions of the First Sweatlodge, which indicates that the sweatlodge is important to them. Here are three of them.

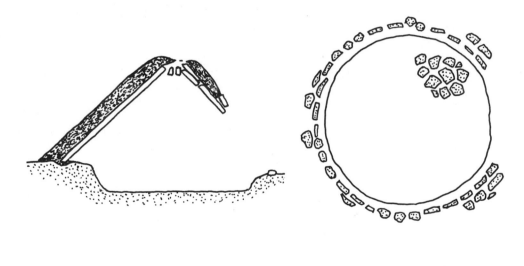

Where the World Began

In the days just after the people emerged from the underworld, Begochidi, or One Who Made Everything, called a meeting of all the people to plan how to live together in the best way. He asked the people but got no response at all. Tired of waiting for suggestions from them, he finally said, "Let us build a sweatlodge for cleansing and purification."

"But we have nothing to make it from," protested the people.

"I will help you," replied One Who Made Everything, and he started to give instructions.

He told First Man to borrow some sticks from Beaver. Then he told him to borrow rocks from Mountain Sheep, fire from Firefly, and water from the daughter of Otter. The people began singing. They sang of wood and of rocks on the wood. Then they sang of fire under the wood and of water in which to bathe. As they sang, they began building the first sweatlodge.

When the people had finished the lodge, they laid Rainbows from the roof and carefully placed the Robe of Darkness over the Rainbows. More rocks were then placed in the center of the lodge. When they had finished the structure, they turned and asked One Who Made Everything what they should use to cover the doorway.

One Who Made Everything replied, "Go and ask grandfather Owl what to use for a door covering."

Now Owl had many robes to offer, and he told the people to chose what they wished. He had flashing robes; white, blue, yellow, and black robes; and sparkling robes. The people chose a flashing robe for the door covering.

Then all the people went into the sweatlodge and sang. They sang of the fire, the stones, the wood, the water, and the flashing robe; they all sang about the heat; then they sang songs of thanks to those who had provided the materials to make the sweatlodge.

When they were finished, they came out of the sweatlodge. One Who Made Everything told them to rub themselves with sand. As they did this, they sang a song of thanks to the earth. Then Locust told them all to go back into the sweatlodge and he would sing for them. He sang them a song of the emergence of the people from the underworld.

The people came out of the sweatlodge a second time and bathed in water left for them by the daughter of Otter. When they were clean, they returned to the lodge to plan the building of the mountains on the earth. These they placed where we see them today and they named them. When the people had made mountains and placed them around the earth, they planned and made the sun, moon, stars, and constellations and placed them in the sky where they belonged. And then the people planned the months.

When they came out of the sweatlodge, they built a hogan of Rainbows for the Six Gods of the people, the Yei gods, and the chiefs. This hogan was used for a big Council. While the Council was meeting, the people sang the Creation Song, "Beginning of the World."

First Man and the Sweatlodge

It is said that First Man made the first sweatlodge. As he climbed up the hollow reed into this world from the Fourth World, he became very dirty. He was covered with mud and smelled like Coyote. Water washed off some of the mud, but left him smelling like Coyote.

Firefly offered to show him how to build a sweatlodge. "Fire God has sent me to instruct you in building and using a sweatlodge to purify and cleanse yourself. Then I will show you how to start a fire to heat the rocks."

First Man thanked Firefly and carefully followed his instructions in building the sweatlodge. Then he watched as Firefly rested a brittle stalk from the beeweed, a summer flower that grows along the roadside, on a small notch in a piece of dry wood. Then he whirled the spindle a few turns. "Now you try it. I will help," said Firefly.

First Man took the spindle and rotated it steadily and surely, as he had seen Firefly work the device. The friction began turning the end of the beeweed into dust. In less than a minute, smoke began to rise from the small mound of dust that was forming. Firefly ignited the dust with a spark from the fire that Fire God had given him. Soon First Man had a good fire going. He used the fire to heat his sweatlodge stones.

First Woman was also dirty and smelled bad after she had climbed into this world from below. After First Man used the sweatlodge, she tried it, too. Ever since, women have used the sweatlodge like the men, but never with them.

Sun Tests the Twins

According to this story, Sun Father made the first sweatlodge when he tested his sons, Monster Slayer and Born For Water, the twin helpers and protectors of the Navajo people. These mischievous boys are very like the Twins of Pueblo mythology, and were probably derived in part from the Pueblo stories.

When Monster Slayer and Born For Water reached the house of the Sun, they called him father, as their mother had instructed. But Sun did not accept them and even thrust a spear at the boys and told them to go away. Sun was surprised to see the spear bounce off both of them as if it were merely a toy. Though Sun could not see it under their shirts, each of the boys wore a magic feather mantle their mother had given them. Neither spears nor arrows could pierce them.

"Perhaps you are my sons," said Sun, looking them over carefully. Moon, however, taunted the boys and filled Sun's mind with strong doubts about them.

"I'm not yet sure, that is true," said Sun. "But I know another test." Sun made four sweatlodges from a substance like iron and placed one in each of the four directions. Then he sent Moon to light a fire near each of them. Moon took the fire from comets, which the Navajo call burning stars. After the sweatlodges became extremely hot, Sun grabbed the boys and placed them in each sweatlodge in turn — east, south, west, and north. Instead of weakening in the fierce heat, the boys actually grew stronger and more vigorous after each sweatlodge visit.

Sun was finally convinced that these two were indeed his sons. He welcomed them and gave the elder twin a powerful bow and arrows, which Monster Slayer used to rid the world of the evil monsters that were plaguing the people. Born For Water helped his brother by scalping the monsters and tying the scalps to his waist.

As the Navajo say, this story shows why you should use the sweatlodge frequently. It invigorates a person for hard work and refreshes him after the work is done.

Sweathouse and the Coming of People

The Nez Perce, from the Plateau region in what is now Idaho and western Oregon, lived in tipis and made their living by hunting, fishing, and gathering wild plants. They were excellent horsemen and raised the highly prized Appaloosa breed of horses, well known by the distinctive white markings on their rumps.

Extremely friendly to the early white explorers and travelers in their country, the Nez Perce helped to guide the Lewis and

Clark expedition as it made its way across the Northwest Rockies. Later, as white settlers began to force them into smaller and smaller hunting grounds, and finally demanded that they move out of the fertile Wallowa valley in northeastern Oregon, the Nez Perce began to fight back. The noble and clever Chief Joseph led his people against four armies. They fought bravely, but the odds were against them and eventually they lost. They were forcibly removed to Indian Territory in Oklahoma, far from their homeland. Today only a few Nez Perce survive in western Idaho.

The Nez Perce sweathouse was very much like that of their Sanpoil neighbors to the northwest. It was a low structure made from saplings bent to form a series of arches, and covered with bark, earth, and grass.

Back when animals were people, there were no human beings — except for one man, Sweathouse. Sweathouse was very wise and had powers that others did not have. One day, he had a vision of the coming of human beings to the world. He could see that these new people would come to dominate the world. Before they came, Sweathouse called a great assembly of the animal people.

When everyone was gathered together, Sweathouse stood up to speak. "I have called you all here today to make an important announcement. I have foreseen the coming of humans to our land. They are men and women and will look as I do. We have lived here in relative peace and quiet for a very long time, and now it is time to share this earth with others."

Sweathouse again paused and took a long, slow breath. "We can no longer live the way we have become accustomed to living. We must part and go to different places to ready the earth for the new people. Each of you must decide what you want to be. Do you want to fly, crawl, run, or swim? What kind of animal do you wish to be?"

There was general murmuring among the animals and then all eyes turned back to Sweathouse. Elk stepped forward and said proudly, "I wish to remain an elk. I do not want to change."

Sweathouse told him to run or gallop to prove to everyone that he was indeed an elk. The large animal galloped off in a large circle around the gathering, then back to stand before Sweathouse.

"You are certainly an elk," said Sweathouse. Elk galloped off again and the others saw no more of him.

Next, Sweathouse called Eagle before him. He asked Eagle, "And what do you want to be?" Eagle said, "I want to stay just what I am — an eagle." With this he flew off, soaring higher and higher in widening circles, hardly seeming to move his wings at all. After a few minutes, he returned and settled before Sweathouse.

"No one flies the way you do, Eagle. An eagle you will remain. You will be king of all the birds and the new humans will admire you always." Eagle flew off and everyone watched as he got smaller and smaller. When they could no longer see him, they turned back to Sweathouse.

Blue Jay hopped up to Sweathouse and squawked shrilly, "I want to be an eagle, too! I can fly just like Eagle." With these words, he flew off, awkwardly flapping his wings. When he tried to soar like Eagle, he tumbled down close to the earth. After a few minutes, he flew to a nearby tree and fluttered and hopped down to stand before Sweathouse.

"You are no eagle," said Sweathouse. "You are a jay and a jay you will always remain." Everyone laughed to see Blue Jay's long face at this news. Blue Jay flew off.

Then Bear came and stood before Sweathouse. "You will remain a bear and will be wild and fierce. You will kill to eat flesh, and humans will respect and fear you." Bear ambled off slowly into the woods.

Sweathouse continued to give the animals names and each scattered to his or her own chosen home.

Finally, only Coyote was left standing before Sweathouse.

"You have been great in your time, Coyote. You are wise and cunning and your name shall last forever. Now, what do you want to be?"

It didn't take Coyote long to answer. "I want to be noble and brave like Cougar, Elk, or Eagle. I do not want to be Coyote any longer." Coyote set off to show Sweathouse what he could do. First, he tried to fly like Eagle, but he only hopped about. He stirred up a lot of dust and finally fell flat on his face.

Not to be daunted, Coyote tried to growl fiercely like Cougar, but he only howled and barked. Then he set off at a gallop, trying to imitate Elk. Truth be told, he did gallop for a short while before returning to his own loping gait. He stopped and looked back at Sweathouse.

"You look just exactly like yourself, foolish Coyote." Sweathouse laughed. "You must be satisfied to stay a coyote." Coyote ran off, barking and whining. When he reached the edge of the forest, he stopped and turned and stood looking at Sweathouse over his shoulder before dashing off again — just exactly the way you see coyotes do today.

That left Sweathouse all alone with no one to talk to but himself. "Well now," he said to himself. "The new humans will be here soon and there is nothing here for them. There should be something to give them strength, hope, and power.

"I will plant myself on the ground for the humans to use when they come. When they come to visit me, I will give them power. I will make them strong in war and great in peace. I will make them great hunters and fishermen. I will heal their ills and protect them from things they fear."

After he had spoken, Sweathouse lay on the ground to wait for the first people. He is still there today, giving power to all who seek it from him.

Glossary

Acoma (AK-o-mah)
Pueblo tribe southwest of Albuquerque, NM

Alkuntam (all-KUN-tam)
Creator god of the Bella Coola

Apache (a-PATCH-e)
Tribe living in central New Mexico and Arizona

Arapaho (a-RAP-a-ho)
Tribe of the Northwestern Plains in what is now southern Wyoming and northern Colorado

Arikara (a-RIK-a-ra)
Tribe of the Northern Plains in what is now North Dakota

Atotarho (a-to-TAR-ho)
Evil being of Iroquois mythology, vanquished by Deganawidah and Hayenwatha

avanyuts (av-AN-yuts)
Mohave name for the willow covering on roof thatch

avapete (av-a-PET-e)
Mohave name for the door to a house

avatsusive (av-a-TSUS-ive)
Mohave name for roof thatching

avatsutara (av-a-TSUS-tar-a)
Mohave name for roof poles

avulypo (av-ul-EE-po)
Mohave name for house posts

Begochidi (beh-GO-chi-dee)
Navajo god, the One Who Made Everything

Bella Coola (BELL-a COO-la)
Northwest Coast tribe of central British Columbia, Canada

Booksta (BOOK-stah)
A Bella Coola character who lay in front of the door of grizzly bear's house prior to a potlatch

Cayuga (kai-YOU-ga)
Tribe of the Iroquois Confederacy living in western New York State

Chaui (CHOW-ee)
A band of the Pawnee Indians

Chemehuevi (CHEM-e-WAVE-y)
A subgroup of the Paiute tribe that live in southern California west of the Colorado River

Cheyenne (shy-ANN)
Northern Plains tribe living in eastern Wyoming and western Nebraska

Chumash (CHOO-mash)
Southern California tribe that lived in the area now occupied by the coastal city of Santa Barbara

Corona Borealis (kuh-ROW-na bow-ree-ALICE)
Early summer constellation (the Northern Crown)

Daqtlawedi (DAKT-la-wed-ee)	Clan of the Tlinqit Indians
Deganawidah (de-GAN-a-wee-dah)	Iroquois folk hero, who guided the establishment of the Iroquois nation
dentalium (den-TAL-ium)	A seashell used by several California tribes as money
Dineh (dee-NEH)	Navajo name for the Navajo tribe
Estoneapesta (es-TONE-a-PES-ta)	Blackfoot name for the Cold Maker, who brings snow, blizzards, and cold weather
Ganhada (gan-HA-da)	Clan of the Tsimshian Indians
Gaxa (GAX-a)	Brother-in-law of Natsihlanae
Haida (HIGH-da)	Tribe living along the coast of British Columbia, Canada
Hawennihyoh (ha-WEN-nee-yo)	Iroquois creator
Hayenwatha (HI-en-wath-ah)	Iroquois folk hero who helped Deganawidah establish the Iroquois nation
Hidatsa (hi-DAT-sa)	Plains tribe living in central North Dakota
hogan (HO-gan)	Traditional Navajo winter dwelling
Hopi (HOE-pee)	Pueblo tribe living in north-central Arizona
Iatiku (ee-AT-ee-ku)	Ancestor of the Acoma people; elder sister to Nautsiti
igumnau (ee-GUM-now)	Mohave name for roof support beams
Iroquois (EAR-uh-kwoi)	Confederacy of tribes that lived in western and northern New York, consisting of the Cayuga, Mohawk, Oneida, Onondaga, and Seneca groups
Isleta (is-LET-a)	Pueblo tribe near the Rio Grande in central New Mexico
Jemez (HAY-mez)	Pueblo tribe living in north-central New Mexico
Kamalsonx (KAH-mal-sonx)	Bella Coola ancestor
Keethit (KEET-hit)	Tlingit ancestral house
Kiowa (KAI-oh-wah)	Southwestern Plains tribe living in western Oklahoma and northern Texas

Kwakiutl (KWA-key-ou-dle)	Northwest Coast tribe living on the islands of western British Columbia, Canada
Lenape (LEN-a-pay)	Also known as the Delaware, a tribe that lived between the Hudson and Delaware rivers until they retreated west beginning in the eighteenth century
Loo'looe (LOO LOO-ee)	White-footed mouse, in a Miwok story about the theft of fire
Maidu (MY-du)	A northern California tribe
Mandan (MAN-dan)	Western Plains Sioux tribe residing in North Dakota
Mastamho (mas-tahm-HO)	The youngest of two brother gods; said to have brought crafts and other knowledge to the Mohave Indians
Matavilya (ma-ta-VIL-ya)	Older brother
Miwok (MI-wok)	A north-central California tribe
Mohave (mo-HAV-ay)	A tribe living along the Colorado River in southern California
Mohawk (MOW-hawk)	Western New York State tribe; a member of the Iroquois Confederacy
Nagunaks (na-GUN-aks)	Tsimshian supernatural being who lived under the sea
Natsihlanae (NAT-sih-lanae)	Ancestor of the Whale-House people, a Tlingit clan
Nautsiti (NAU-tsit-ee)	Ancestor of the Acoma Indians; younger sister of Iatiku
Navajo (NAV-a-ho)	Southwestern tribe living in northeastern Arizona, northwestern New Mexico, and southern Utah; the largest North American tribe
Nez Perce (nez PURSE)	Tribe living in the Plateau region of Idaho and western Oregon
Nimkish (NIM-kish)	Clan of the Kwakiutl Indians
Nomlaki (nom-LAHK-ee)	Indian tribe of central California
nusmata (NOOSE-mah-ta)	Bella Coola House of Myths
Nusqalst (NOOSE-callst)	Ancient Bella Coola village

Oneida (oh-NYE-da)	Tribe residing in western New York State; a member of the Iroquois Confederacy
Onondaga (ON-on-dag-a)	Tribe residing in western New York State; a member of the Iroquois Confederacy
Palonqwhoya (pa-LONG-kwa-hoy-a)	The younger of the Hopi Twins, helpers and protectors of the Hopi people
Papago (PAP-a-go)	Tribe living in southern Arizona
parfleche (PAR-flesh)	A rawhide with the hair removed
Paruxti (par-UX-ti)	Pawnee god, the Wonderful Being, spokesman for Tirawahat
Pawnee (paw-NEE)	Plains tribe of central Nebraska
Pima (PEEM-a)	Tribe living in southern Arizona
Pomo (PO-mo)	North-central California tribe
Poqangwhoya (po-KANGW-hoy-a)	Eldest of the Hopi Twins, helpers and protectors of the Hopi people
Pueblo (PWEB-low)	Tribes living along the Rio Grande in New Mexico, western New Mexico (Zuni) and north-central Arizona (Hopi)
Quinault (KIN-alt)	Northwest Coast tribe living west of what is now Seattle
Sagodyowehgowah (sa-GODE-ee-o-way-go-wah)	Ancestor of the Iroquois False Face Society
Salish (SALE-ish)	Northwest Coast tribe living west of what is now Seattle
Sanpoil (SAN-poil)	Tribe living in central Washington state
Seneca (SEN-eh-ka)	Westernmost of the Iroquois tribes; from New York; member of the Iroquois Confederacy
Senx (SENX)	Bella Coola sun god; he lived in the House of Myths
Sioux (SOO)	Indian tribe of the Central Plains
sipapu (see-pah-PU)	Hopi name for the place of emergence from the underworld
Skidi (SKEE-dee)	Wolf band of the Pawnee tribe
Slo'w (SLO)	A Chumash sky god who was a golden eagle

Tirawahat (TIR-ah-wah-hut)	Pawnee supreme spirit
Tlingit (TLING-it)	Tribe living on the islands of northwestern British Columbia, Canada
Tsichtinako (tsi-CHIN-ah-ko)	Acoma creator goddess
Tsimshian (TSIM-shi-an)	Northwest coast tribe who live in British Columbia, north of Vancouver Island
Tsu-Suc-Cub (TSU-SUC-CUB)	Name of an historic house of the Coast Salish
Walapai (WAL-ah-pie)	Tribe of west central Arizona
Wetskak (WETS-kak)	Name of the smallest dentalium shell
Wintu (WIN-too)	Indian people of Sacramento River area, northern California
Xoy (ZOY)	Chumash supernatural being of the sky world
Yavapai (YA-va-pie)	A tribe of central Arizona related to the Walapai
Yurok (YUR-ok)	Northern California tribe
Yei (YEA)	Navajo name for their gods
Zuñi (ZOO-nee)	Pueblo tribe living in western New Mexico

Suggested Further Reading

Bierhorst, John. *The Mythology of North America*. New York: Morrow, 1985.

Caduto, Michael J., and Joseph Bruchac. *Keepers of the Earth: Native American Stories and Environmental Activities for Children*. Golden, Colo.: Fulcrum, Inc., 1988.

Clark, Ella E. *Indian Legends of the Pacific Northwest*. Berkeley: University of California Press, 1975.

Clark, Ella E. *Indian Legends from the Northern Rockies*. Norman: University of Oklahoma Press, 1966.

Curtis, Edward S. *The Girl Who Married a Ghost and Other Tales from the North American Indian*. New York: Four Winds Press, 1978.

Curtis, Natalie. *The Indians' Book*. New York: Crown, 1986.

Cushing, Frank H. *Zuni Folk Tales*. Tucson: University of Arizona Press, 1986.

Erdoes, Richard, and Alfonso Ortiz, eds. *American Indian Myths and Legends*. New York: Pantheon Books, 1985.

Feldman, Susan, ed. *The Story-Telling Stone: Myths and Tales of the American Indians*. New York: Dell Publishing Co., 1965.

Fisher, Anne B. *Stories California Indians Told*. Berkeley: Parnassus Press, 1957.

Gifford, Edward W., and Gwendoline Harris Block. *Californian Indian Nights*. Lincoln: University of Nebraska Press, 1990.

Grinnell, George B. *By Cheyenne Campfires*. Lincoln: University of Nebraska Press, 1971.

Hayes, Joe. *Coyote &*. Santa Fe, N.M.: Mariposa Publishing, 1983.

Kroeber, Theodora. *The Inland Whale*. Berkeley: University of California Press, 1959.

Lankford, George E., ed. *Native American Legends*. Little Rock, Ark.: August House, 1987.

Marriott, Alice Lee. *Winter-telling Stories*. New York: Crowell, 1969.

Marriott, Alice Lee. *Dance Around the Sun*. New York: Crowell, 1977.

Marriott, Alice, and Carol K. Rachlin. *American Indian Mythology*. New York: Crowell, 1969.

Marriott, Alice, and Carol K. Rachlin. *Plains Indian Mythology*. New York: Crowell, 1975.

Mayo, Gretchen Will. *Star Tales*. New York: Walker Publishing Co., Inc., 1987.

Monroe, Jean Guard, and Ray A. Williamson. *They Dance in the Sky: Native American Star Myths*. Boston: Houghton Mifflin, 1987.

Mourning Dove. *Coyote Stories*. Lincoln: University of Nebraska Press, 1990.

Mullet, G. M. *Spider Woman Stories*. Tucson: University of Arizona Press, 1979.

Ramsey, Jarold. *Coyote Was Going There: Indian Literature of the Oregon Country*. Seattle and London: University of Washington Press, 1977.

Rose, Anne K. *Spider in the Sky*. New York: Harper & Row, 1978.

Thompson, Stith. *Tales of the North American Indians*. Bloomington and London: University of Indiana Press, 1966.

Turner, Frederick W., III, ed. *The Portable North American Indian Reader*. New York: Viking Press, 1973.

Williamson, Ray. *Living the Sky: The Cosmos of the American Indian*. Boston: Houghton Mifflin, 1984.

Bibliography

General Information

Nabokov, Peter, and Robert Easton. *Native American Architecture*. Oxford: Oxford University Press, 1989. Williamson, Ray A. *Living the Sky: The Cosmos of the American Indian*. Boston: Houghton Mifflin, 1984.

The People of the Longhouse: The Iroquois League

Cornplanter, Jesse J. *Legends of the Longhouse*. Port Washington, N.Y.: Ira J. Friedman, 1963, pp. 206–8. Hewitt, J.N.B. "Legend of the Founding of the Iroquois League," *American Anthropologist* 5 (1892): 131–48.

General Information: Graymont, Barbara. *The Iroquois*. New York: Chelsea House Publishers, 1988. Hertzberg, Hazel. *The Great Tree and the Longhouse: The Culture of the Iroquois*. New York: Macmillan, 1966. Parker, Arthur C. *Parker on the Iroquois*, William N. Fenton, ed. Syracuse: Syracuse University Press, 1968. Wallace, Paul H. *The White Roots of Peace*. Port Washington, N.Y.: Ira J. Friedman, 1968.

A Gift of the Gods: The Navajo Hogan

O'Bryan, Aileen. "The Diné: Origin Myths of the Navaho Indians." *Smithsonian Institution Bureau of American Ethnology Bulletin* 16 (1956). Wyman, Leland C. *Blessingway*. Tucson: University of Arizona Press, 1970, p. 15.

General Information: Louis, Ray Baldwin. *Child of the Hogan*. Provo: Brigham Young University Press, 1975. Newcomb, Franc J. *Navaho Folktales*. Santa Fe: Ancient City Press, 1989. Jett, Stephen C., and V. E. Spencer. *Navaho Architecture*. Tucson, University of Arizona Press, 1981.

Emergence from the Underworld: The Pueblo Kiva

Benedict, Ruth. *Zuni Mythology*. New York: Columbia University Press, 1935. Stirling, Matthew W. "Origin Myth of Acoma." *Smithsonian Institution Bureau of American Ethnology Bulletin* 135 (1942): 19–20.

General Information: Scully, Vincent. *Pueblo: Mountain, Village, Dance*. New York: Viking Press, 1975. Yue, Charlotte and David. *The Pueblo*. Boston: Houghton Mifflin, 1986.

Shade and Shelter: Mohave Houses

Kroeber, A. L. "Seven Mohave Myths." *University of California Anthropological Records* 11 (1948): 56–57.

Index

Acoma Indians, 28, 35–38
Alaska, 72, 81
Alkuntam, 77–78, 79, 80
Anasazi Indians, 36
Apache Indians, 128
Arapaho Indians, 96, 99–100
  Buffalo Lodge ceremony,
  101–5
Arikara Indians, 106
Arizona, 18, 28, 39
Assembly houses (Miwok),
  55–57
Atotarho, 9–16

Baexolla, 77–78
Beate (prophet), 119–20
Begochidi, 131
Bella Coola Indians, vii,
  77–78
Bella Coola River, 79
Big House (Delaware Indi-
  ans), x, 120–22
Blackfoot Indians, 90–100
  Snow Tipi myth, 92–95
  tipis, 90–100
Booksta, 80
British Columbia, 77, 79,
  126
Buffalo, 93, 96
  Ceremony, 101–5
  hunts, 107
  paintings of, 92
  rites, 116
  in Snow Tipi myth, 92–
  93, 94
  spirit of, 114

California, x, 39
California Indians
  Chumash, 48–55, 60

house myths, 47–68
  Miwok, 55–60
  Sun's Crystal House
  myth, 50–55
  Yurok, 60–68
Canada, 119
Cannibalism, 8, 77–78
Cayuga tribe, 1
Chaui Band (Pawnee), 113
Chemehuevi Indians, 42, 44
Cherokee Indians, viii
Cheyenne Indians, 96
Chief Joseph, 135
Chumash Indians, 48–55, 60
Colorado River, 39–40, 42
Condolence Ceremony, 16
Corn Mother, 2
Corona Borealis, 112
Creation myths, vii
  animals in, 58
  Lenape, 120
  Mojave, 41–44
  Navajo, 18–21
  Pueblo, 28–29
Creation Song, 132
Creek Indians, viii
Crow Indians, 96

Daqtlawedi Clan, 83
Decoration, house
  carvings, 70, 71, 75, 81
  paintings, 70, 71, 72, 81,
  84, 92, 93
  tipi, 91–92, 94–95, 99–100
Deganawidah, 10–16
Delaware (state), 118
Delaware Indians, 118–19
  Big House Annual Cere-
  mony, x, 120–22
  longhouses, 119

Delaware River, 118
Dineh ("The People"), 18
Diseases, viii, 48–49, 69,
  107

Earth lodges (Pawnee), 106,
  107, 109
  design/construction, viii,
  113–15
  First Earth Lodge myth,
  112–17
  stone, 108–9
Estoneapesta, 94, 95
European(s)
  diseases brought by, viii,
  48–49, 69, 107
  settlements, vii, 3, 107

False Face Society myth,
  4–7
Fire myth, 57–60
Fir Mountain, 24

Ganhada clan, 84–85
Gaxa, 82, 83
Gold, 55
Great Dark House, 42
Great Manitou, 120
Great Tree, The, 11, 13
Green Corn Festival, 2

Haida Indians, 72
Hawennihyoh, 6–7
Hayenwatha, 9–11
Hidatsa Indians, 96, 106
Hogan of Rainbows, 132
Hogans (Navajo), vii, ix,
  17–26
  design/construction, viii,
  22, 24, 25

First Hogan myth, 21–25
Sky Hogan myth, 25–26
Hopi Indians, 28–29
  Sun Father's House myth, 31–35
Horses, 98, 134
Hudson River, 8
Husk Faces, 4–7

Iatiku, 35, 36–38
Idaho, 134
Iroquois Indians, 1–3, 119
  League, 8–16
  longhouses, vii, viii, 12
  Nation, 14, 16
  sacred masks myths, 4–7
  trail, 8–9
Isleta Indians, 28

Jemez Indians, 28

Kachinas, 36, 38
Kamalsonx, 79–80
Kansas, 107
Keethit (Killer-Whale House), 81–84
Killer-Whale House people, 81–84
Kiowa Indians, 96
Kiva (Pueblo), 27–28
  design/construction, 36–37
  First Kiva myth, 35–38
Klamath River, 60
Kwakiutl Indians, 75–77

Lenape Indians, 118, 120
Lewis and Clark, 134–35
Longhouses (Delaware), 119
Longhouses (Iroquois), vii, viii, 1
  design/construction, 3–4
  purpose, 8–9

Loo'looe, 58–59
Loop River, 107

Maidu Indians, 57
Mandan Indians, 106
Mastamho, 41–44, 45–46
Matavilya, 42, 46
Missouri River, 106
Miwok Indians, 55–60
Mohawk tribe, 1, 8
Mojave Indians, x, 39–41, 42, 48
  Beginning Time myths, 41
  ramadas, vii, 41–44, 45
  winter houses, 44–46
Munsee band, 120
Murie, James R., 116–17
Myths and storytelling, ix–x, 57

Nagunaks (Chief of the Sea), 86–89
Natsihlanae, 81–83
Nautsiti, 35, 38
Navajo Indians, x, 17–18, 28
  emergence myth, 18–21
  hogans, vii, viii, ix, 17–26
  Reservation, 18
  sweatlodges, 128, 130–34
Nebraska, 107
New Jersey, 118
New Mexico, 18, 28, 35
New York (state), 118
Nez Perce Indians, 134–37
Nimkish tribe, 76
Nomlaki Indians, 57
Northwest Coast Indians, viii, x
  Bella Coola, 77–78, 79
  houses, 69–73
  Kwakiutl, 75–77
  potlatch ceremony, 78–81
  Quinault, 73–75

Sea-Raven House myth, 84–85
Tlingit, 72, 81–84
Tsimshian, 72, 84–89
Nusmata (House of Myths), 77–78, 79, 80
Nusqalst myth, 79–80

Oklahoma, 108, 119, 122, 135
Ohio, 19
Omaha Indians, 106
Oñate, Juan de, 40
Oneida tribe, 1
Onondaga tribe, 1, 9
Oregon, 134, 135
Oto Indians, 106

Palonqwhoya, 32
Paruxti, 112, 113–15, 116
Pawnee Indians
  earth lodges, viii, 106, 107, 108–9, 113–15
  First Earth Lodge myth, 112–17
  Morning Star Bundle myth, 108–12
  Thunder Ritual, 116
Pennsylvania, 119
Plains Indians
  Arapaho, 96, 99–100, 101–5
  Blackfoot, 90–100
  dances and ceremonies, ix
  earth lodges, 106–17
  Pawnee, 106–17
  tipis, ix–x, 90–105, 106, 107
Platte River, 107
Pomo Indians, 57
Ponca Indians, 106
Poquagwhoya, 32
Potlatch ceremony, 78–81
Pueblo Indians, vii, x, 27–28, 133

Center or Middle Place myth, 29–31
creation myth, 28–29
First Kiva myth, 35–38
Sun Father's House myth, 31–35
Puget Sound, 73

Quinault Indians, 73–75

Ramadas (Mojave), vii, 41–44, 45
Rio Grande, 28
Roundhouses, 57, 58–59

Sacramento River, 55
Sagodyowehgowah, 6–7
Salish Indians, 72, 73, 74
San Joaquin River, 55
Sanpoil Indians, 124–25, 126, 135
Santa Clara Indians, 28
Seneca tribe, 1, 8
Senx, 77–78
Sioux Indians, viii, 96, 107
Six Gods, 132
Six Songs, 11, 13, 14
Skidi Band (Pawnee), 107, 108–12
Southeastern tribes, viii
Southwest, vii, 27, 36
sweatlodges, 128
Spanish explorers, 27, 40
animals brought by, 28, 98

diseases brought by, viii, 48–49, 69, 107
Stars
constellations, 91, 94, 112, 116
Milky Way, 36, 120
Morning Star Bundle myth, 108–12
Sun Dance (Plains Indians), ix, 90–91
Sweatlodges, x, 123–24
Blue Jay and Sweatlodge myth, 126–28
Chief Sweatlodge myth, 125
design and construction, 61, 124, 128–30, 135
First Sweatlodge myth, 128–34
Miwok, 55
in Sky Condor myth, 62, 63
women in, 133
Yurok, 61–62, 67

Thompson Indians, 126–28
Tipis, ix–x, 106, 109
Blackfoot, 90–100
decorations, 91–92, 94–95, 99–100
design and construction, 95–100
Nez Perce, 134
Sioux, viii
Snow Tipi myth, 92–95

Tirawahat, 108–9, 112, 113, 114, 115, 117
Tlingit Indians, 72, 81–84
Trade routes, 107
Traveling Rite, 5
Tree of Peace, 14–15, 16
Tsichtinako, 35, 36
Tsimshian Indians, 72
Nagunaks myth, 86–89
Sea-Raven House myth, 84–86

Utah, 18

Vancouver, George, 72
Vancouver Island, 75
Vasquez de Coronado, Francisco, 27

Walapai Indians, 42, 44
Wampum, 11, 13–14, 16
Washington, 73
Werskak, 67–68
Wintu Indians, 57

Xoy, 51

Yavapai, 42, 44
Yei gods, 132
Yurok Indians, 60
houses, 65–68
Sky Condor myth, 61–65

Zuni Indians, 28–29
Center or Middle Place myth, 29–31